CONCEPT DEVELOPMENT IN THE PRIMARY SCHOOL

CONCEPT
DEVELOPMENT
IN THE
Primary
School

PETER LANGFORD

CROOM HELM
London • New York • Sydney

© 1987 Peter Langford
Croom Helm Ltd, Provident House, Burrell Row,
Beckenham, Kent, BR3 1AT
Croom Helm Australia, 44-50 Waterloo Road,
North Ryde, 2113, New South Wales

Published in the USA by
Croom Helm
in association with Methuen, Inc.
29 West 35th Street
New York, NY 10001

British Library Cataloguing in Publication Data

Langford, Peter
    Concept development in the primary school.
    1. Education (Elementary) 2. Cognition
    (Child psychology)
    I. Title
    370.15′2   LB1139.C/   *6 0 3 6 3 3 1 1*
    ISBN 0-7099-4162-5

Library of Congress Cataloging-in-Publication Data

Langford, Peter.
    Concept development in the primary school.

    Bibliography: p.
    Includes index.
    1. Thought and thinking — Study and teaching (Primary)
2. Cognition in children. I. Title.
LB1590.3.L36   1987   371.1′02   87-13733
ISBN 0-7099-4162-5

Jacket photograph is reproduced by courtesy of Sally and Richard Greenhill.

Laser printing by Dead Set Publishing and Information Services Ltd,
169 Bourke Street, Melbourne, Australia

Printed and bound in Great Britain
by Billing & Sons Limited, Worcester.

CONTENTS

Chapter 1: Introduction   1

General orientation, descriptive changes in cognitive abilities, the problem of working memory, how children learn concepts, learning in the primary classroom.

Chapter 2: Reading   15

The reading process and learning to read, conceptions of story, concepts of print, reading strategies.

Chapter 3: Writing   28

The writing process and learning to write, the development of overall organisation, egocentrism, coding and audiences.

Chapter 4: Art   36

Children's representational painting and drawing, non-representational painting and drawing, does art help children to think?

Chapter 5: Science   54

Classification, causality, children's physics.

Chapter 6: Mathematics   76

Conservation, number concepts, the number system, learning arithmetic.

Bibliography   101

Index   130

Chapter 1

INTRODUCTION

GENERAL ORIENTATION

The aim of this book is to introduce the primary teacher to recent work in the area of cognitive development that is relevant to the interests of the classroom practitioner. The field of cognitive development is one that has changed quite considerably in recent years and it is as well to be aware of the general nature of these changes.

For many years the best known work in the area was that of the Swiss psychologist Jean Piaget (1896-1980). From the publication of his first book *The Language and Thought of the Child* in 1926 until his death in 1980 Piaget published over forty books and innumerable journal articles on cognitive development in children. His leading idea was that the child's thinking moves through stages of increasingly abstract concepts until it reaches adulthood. He outlined three main stages in development: the sensorimotor stage from 0 to about 2 years, during which the child's thinking is closely tied to practical activity; the stage of concrete operations, from about 2-11 years of age, during which children think about what is physically possible, such as adding together objects or altering the world by moving things around, lifting them up, stretching them or otherwise subjecting them to transformation; and finally the stage of formal operations from about 11 years onward, in which the adolescent learns to think about purely abstract entities like geometrical points and lines, to understand mathematical functions and how to control factors in an experimental situation.

Piaget also believed that children's thinking develops primarily as a result of their activity in the world in making things, altering situations and transforming objects. It was partly as a result of this Piagetian emphasis on learning through doing that primary schools in the UK began to adopt 'activity methods' of teaching in the 1930s in which children were encouraged to explore the natural environment in a practical way, to undertake projects and to learn mathematics by using practical apparatus enabling them to count collections of objects and observe relationships between objects. In the 1950s and 1960s this adoption of activity methods became widespread and also migrated into secondary schools, although even in the 1970s surveys showed that many primary schools continued to emphasise paper and pencil activities rather than practical work and projects.[1]

Piaget's ideas were never without their critics within psychology and education. In the 1930s many of the criticisms aired in more recent years received publicity.[2] However Piaget persisted with the main elements of his theory, though continually breaking new ground in his study of specific topics and the details of their treatment. In the 1960s his ideas gained new popularity both in the UK and the USA. In academic psychology the 1950s produced the 'cognitive revolution'. Behaviouristic psychology's emphasis on 'rats and stats' and the formation of habits and its neglect of thinking and higher mental processes began to be challenged. A professional joke of the time was 'First psychology lost its soul, then it lost its mind'. In this new climate Piaget came to be seen as a kind of hero of the cognitive revolution, who had held out against behaviourism and accumulated a vast store of observations on children's thinking in real-life situations. This at a time when American psychologists of the 1930s had sometimes appeared lost in the mazes along with their rats.

In education the 1960s saw two changes that helped Piaget's cause in that field as well. American education became concerned at the apparent technological lead held by the Russians in space research. It was felt that the education system should devote more of its time to developing the thinking, conceptual understanding and problem solving skills needed by the scientist and engineer. At the same time the youth revolution and 'flower power' of the 1960s led many educators to search for a less rigid and formal view of learning than that which had hitherto dominated educational thinking. Again Piaget seemed to have something to offer.

The three best known alternatives to Piaget within educational psychology in the 1960s, and still to some extent, even today, were all Americans. Bruner, Gagné and Ausubel all proposed alternative views of how children learn during the 1950s and 1960s. Of these, Bruner's views have declined in popularity in recent years, while considerable publicity has been given to both Gagné and Ausubel as promising alternatives to Piaget. For the present I will only comment on the relation between Piaget and Gagné. Ausubel's work will resurface continually throughout the book.

The idea of a hierarchy of skills is crucial to recent discussions of cognitive development. There are two kinds of hierarchy of skills, which we can call expression hierarchies and logical hierarchies. Reading, writing and drawing are examples of expression hierarchies as they involve low-level skills like handwriting, word recognition and skill with a pencil in the service of expressing high level concepts or ideas. Logical hierarchies occur when there is a logical sequence of concepts within a curriculum area, as we find for instance in geometry, where the concept of a straight line logically precedes those of angles or triangles as we need the concept of straight line to define angles and triangles.

It is typical of the Piagetian approach to think that in expression hierarchies learning is top-down. If the child or adolescent get their high-level general concepts sorted out then lower-level skills will automatically fall into place. The way to get the student to understand broad and general concepts is to encourage discovery of basic principles by exposing the learner to situations and materials that will allow them to discover such principles without much assistance from the teacher.

Piaget's contention in regard to logical hierarchies was that such orderings are an illusion produced by taking a logical rather than a psychological approach to development. In his view the various concepts involved in a topic like arithmetic or geometry develop alongside one another rather than in logical sequence, finally achieving logical rigour more or less simultaneously as a new intellectual structure is formed.

Gagné says that for both expression and logical hierarchies the child must begin at the bottom of the hierarchy with low-level skills and work up to more general levels of understanding. The way to do this is to place the child in a highly structured learning programme that teaches the skills to be acquired with a minimum of errors.

To give examples, in the area of writing the Piagetian educator will tend to say that we should concentrate on the topic of the writing, say pigs. Once the child knows all about pigs, their habits, intelligence, usefulness to human beings, food, etc., then ability to write well about pigs will quickly follow. The Gagnéan teacher will say that we should first begin with the skill of letter formation, then practise writing words, then sentences and finally look at information about pigs to help us to write stories about them.

In a curriculum area like geometry the Piagetian teacher will delay instruction until the structure of geometrical thinking has matured, which in the case of Euclidean geometry is not held to occur until early adolescence. The Gagnéan teacher will begin teaching simple concepts like straight line and angle much earlier and use these to gradually develop more advanced geometrical instruction.

The main message of more recent work and classroom experience has been as follows. Firstly, for expression hierarchies there is no general prescription as to whether learning should be 'top-down' or 'bottom-up'. What the child needs to learn in order to develop a given cognitive skill will depend mainly upon the levels at which they are weakest. This may differ from child to child and from area to area. In some areas it may be that most children need more help with low-level skills, in others they may need more help with high-level conceptual understanding.

For logical hierarchies we find that it tends to be true, as alleged by Gagné, that a strictly logical understanding of a topic does require an orderly development from basic concepts to those that are defined with them. However it is both possible and desirable to provide intuitive and pictorial insights into a topic as a whole before proceeding with detailed logical development. In geometry, for instance, we might want to begin by showing examples of how relatively advanced Euclidean geometry can be used in such things as calculating the distance of the sun from the earth or the height of an unclimbable mountain before proceeding to detailed definitions and methods of proof.

Another finding is that there is no single prescription as to how best to learn a given cognitive skill. Children may benefit from exploration, discovery, 'hands on' experience or from being told, from a demonstration or a tightly sequenced programme to develop a specific skill. Most children seem to benefit most from a mixture of these methods. Some generalisations about learning are, however, possible. It is usually better to practise an expression skill like reading or writing as a meaningful whole, even though the student may initially be very weak in all aspects of the skill, than to break up the task into component subskills like handwriting or word recognition and practise these in isolation; though a moderate amount of practice with component skills will be accepted by the student once they have realised where these skills fit into the overall skill of reading or writing. It is, however, desirable to sequence the curriculum in accordance with the logical sequence of concepts, particularly in science and mathematics.

It is always important to keep the student interested and mentally involved in the activity in question. It is important to ensure that the activity does actually practise the skills it claims to practise. Teachers should look very carefully at claims that practice in one area benefits skill in an apparently unrelated area. Direct practice of a skill is always better than transfer from another area.

DESCRIPTIVE CHANGES IN COGNITIVE ABILITIES

Piagetian theory was in some respects rather successful in suggesting the kinds of topics appropriate for primary age children. Piaget called the period from roughly 7-11 years of age the 'substage of concrete operations', which is to say that it is a substage of the broader stage of concrete operations extending from about 2-11 years. By this he meant that in the age range 7-11 children successfully understand the world in terms of operations they can actually perform on it. It is important here to avoid a misunderstanding that beginners often have in approaching Piagetian ideas. 'Concrete operations' does not mean simply understanding what does happen in the world. Even 4 and 5 year old children enjoy stories about dwarfs and giants that they have never seen. They have seen things getting larger and smaller and they can imagine what people would be like if they got larger or smaller. Concrete operations means possible extensions of concrete experiences.

In some ways it would be more realistic to think of 'concrete operations' in this sense as the period from 4-9 years. From 4 years children begin to understand things like arithmetic and logic from a concrete point of view. By 9 years there is already evidence that children can in some circumstances break away from physical reality in their mathematical thinking. Thus Langford (1974) asked children to imagine the number 1, to add 1, then another 1, and so on. When asked 'Would we ever have to stop?' a majority of 9 year olds said 'No', showing that unlike younger children they can imagine going on forever, which is physically impossible but is a concept used by mathematicians. Younger children tend to say 'You would have to stop for lunch' or even 'You would die'!

Given this slight downward revision in the age range, Piaget's idea that children in middle childhood conceive only physically possible operations on the world remains valid. His serious mistakes began when he tried to say a) that there is a sudden overall shift in patterns of thinking at around age 7; b) that these patterns can be described by logically coherent systems called 'grouping structures'. These claims are not widely accepted today.

In addition to this general description of children's thinking from 4-9 we can also add three rather well-established principles that, other things being equal, will determine the difficulty of a concept for a child in this period. Rather than finding the sudden emergence of a whole bundle of concepts what we find instead is the gradual emergence of concepts in a fashion indicated by these principles. The first is that any problem or statement that involves a difficult constituent concept will be difficult.[3] Two examples of difficult constituent concepts are 'not', as in 'Ducks are not mammals', and 'includes', as in 'The class of herbivores includes the class of horses'. A statement involving both concepts, such as 'Cats are not herbivores', will be doubly difficult.

The second principle is that the more complex a statement the more difficult it will be to grasp or operate with.[4] Thus an arithmetical statement like $(2 + 3) \times (6 + 4)$ is more complex than 2×6. No one has ever satisfactorily defined this kind of complexity, but in an intuitive sense we know it when we see it.

The third principle is that any problem or statement that places a greater load on memory will be more difficult to deal with. The upshot of these three principles acting together is that the development of thinking from 4-9 shows a gradual increase in the complexity and memory-taxing powers of the problems and ideas mastered and in the difficulty of constituent concepts that can be tackled. Even after 9 years, although the first truly 'abstract' ideas appear, many of the more complex and difficult principles governing the logic and mathematics of physically possible situations are still not grasped. The process of learning these goes on right through adolescence. We also find that concrete statements like $2 + 3 = 3 + 2$ are understood before rules that apply to such statements, such as the com-

mutative law of addition which says that for any numbers A and B,
$A + B = B + A$.

The finding that cognitive development does not proceed in sudden
leaps has implications for the teacher. It means that we need in most cases
to use methods that allow a student to find their own level rather than allot-
ting them to a level of work on the basis of some rather general label like
'late concrete operations' or 'early formal operations'. Two ways of
achieving this are to use an individualised programme in which the student
works through workbooks and activities that are sequenced in order of
difficulty and allow each student to find their own level; or by allowing for
self-directed learning, as when students choose their own books to read or
their own topics to write about.

THE PROBLEM OF WORKING MEMORY

We have already seen that one of the difficulties that children must overcome is that imposed by limited memory. All cognitive tasks require the
child to hold a certain number of ideas or mental 'items' for a short time in
'working memory' while they are acted upon. This has caused a number of
theorists to think that the main thing holding up the development of
children's thinking is the limitation of this working memory. Examples of
this can be found in Pascual-Leone (1971), Case (1979) and Halford and
Wilson (1980). These three groups of authors have actually suggested that
the working memory capacity of children could be used to provide a new
kind of definition for stages in intellectual development to replace those of
Piaget. Thus children at one stage would have working memory capacity
of two items, at the next stage of three items, and so forth.

There are, however, serious limitations to such approaches. To begin
with, the general idea that working memory limitations are the chief thing
holding up development is not inherently obvious; it is at the outset just as
plausible to think that the problem of learning new ways of processing information — new recognition of concepts, new routines and new strategies — is just as great a source of difficulty for the child. Thus we would
need some kind of empirical proof that it is actually the case that working
memory problems are what holds the child up. While the authors mentioned above do try to provide such evidence, their critics have been less
than totally convinced by the evidence offered.[5] The difficulties are
threefold. It is hard to arrange an independent assessment of the working
memory capacity of a child as we never really know how long information
must be stored in the child's mind during processing. We know that both
adults and children can remember a lot more for only half a second than
they can for say three seconds. Secondly, it is hard to know just how
children chunk information while performing a task. If the child needs to
remember the number 12 for instance this might normally be two items;

on the other hand it might be the child's age or their birthday, in which case 12 will be chunked as 'my age' or 'my birthday'. As working memory load has to be defined in terms of number of chunks stored, this creates a further difficulty. Thirdly there has been dispute about the actual strategies children use to perform the particular tasks studied when testing the models. It is of course likely that limitations on working memory play a partial role in restricting the abilities that young children can acquire, as suggested in the model of solving arithmetical problems proposed by Brainerd (1983). It seems, however, quite premature to conclude that this is the main difficulty restricting performance. If it is not the main difficulty then there is little point in trying to define stages of development using assessments of working memory.

HOW CHILDREN LEARN CONCEPTS

It is rather easy to see how children come by much of what they know: either they have seen it themselves, they have seen a picture of it or they have heard about it. A child may know from its own experience that 'James is a friend of John'; they may have seen a cartoon on TV and know that 'Tom is not a friend of Jerry'; they may have heard the stories about Pooh bear and know that 'Pooh is a friend of Piglet'.

Even this kind of knowing is not as simple as it appears. It would be much easier to judge that 'James is taller than John' than to judge that 'James is a friend of John'. To judge that James is taller than John you just have to get them to stand next to one another. But simply seeing James in some kind of friendly social situation with John does not show they are really friends. The idea of friendship contains a notion of 'is regularly friendly with'. Even quite young children manage to make this kind of judgement. If we ask them 'Who is friends with who?' they may say things like 'Mary is not friends with Jill today' or 'Peter is sort of friends with Diane'. Similarly they know what it means to be a robber or a witch, to be grateful or careless, to be wobbly or in a hurry.

How do children pick up these rather subtle meanings without being told? Most psychologists now explain this as being through a kind of 'hypothesis evaluation'. On hearing mother tell them 'Now you are friends with Bill' the child automatically begins to think of some guess or hypothesis that will explain what this means. Suppose that the two children have just had a fight and made it up. This may lead to the idea that 'friends' means just having had a fight and being friendly again. But the next time the word 'friends' is used may be in the statement 'Would you like to have your friends around today?' This example will tell against the association with fights and perhaps encourage the child to think of friends as children who regularly come to play.

At one time it was popular to think that children are very efficient at evaluating hypotheses of this kind. Most recent research shows, however, that children of less than 11 years are generally rather inefficient in evaluating hypotheses.[6] In particular, if they come upon examples that disprove hypotheses they have formed to explain a situation, they often ignore these counter-examples and retain the original hypothesis. After enough counter-examples they abandon the hypothesis and move on to a better one, but they may need several experiences of disconfirmation to do this. For this reason we can explain much conceptual learning in primary age children as being due to the fact that correct guesses will, in the long run, usually be those that are most often called forth by a given situation. So in the case of learning the concept 'friends' the majority of situations in which this is used will be cases where friendly relations over a period of time are suggested. Situations where friends fight and make it up or where two friends happen to be wearing the same kind of jumper may appear occasionally and lead to temporary misconceptions. But in the long run such ideas will drop out in favour of those suggested more frequently.

To give another example of this kind of learning more closely related to school work, by about 7 years of age most children know that for any two numbers A and B, the commutative law of addition holds such that $A + B$ is always equal to $B + A$. If a child sees that $2 + 3 = 3 + 2$ it may hazard a guess that 'It doesn't matter which order you add them in'. Alternatively it may think 'If one lot of numbers begins with A and the other lot ends with A, then the two totals are the same'. The first idea will always be true, while the second will often be false and so will drop out. If of course a situation regularly suggests a misleading idea then this will also become firmly rooted. An example of this is that most children and adults will predict that if a stone is placed in a bath of mercury it will sink, though many stones will actually float. We have always experienced stones sinking in liquids and think this is always so.

After 11 years of age adolescents are able to evaluate hypotheses more systematically and once a counter-example comes up they can discard their incorrect hypothesis permanently.[7] However, both adolescents and adults operate for much of the time in a 'semi-automatic' state in which they generate hypotheses about situations but don't bother much about implementing strictly logical strategies for eliminating incorrect hypotheses. Thus even as adults many of our ideas continue to be those that have most frequently been suggested by a situation and the occasional counter-example is simply forgotten.

LEARNING IN THE PRIMARY CLASSROOM

Primary teachers try to teach two quite different kinds of conceptual understanding and skill: those involved in communication with others and those involved in thinking about the world. The first kind of teaching is more typical of instruction in reading and writing, the second of instruction in science and mathematics. Piagetian psychology was unusual in that these two kinds of understanding were held to be rather closely linked. Piaget claimed that up to around 7 years the average child is egocentric in communication; that is to say they communicate poorly because they tend to forget that the listener or reader does not know everything they know. At the same time the young child's thinking about the world is limited by being bound to a single point of view. After 7 years both these kinds of limitation are overcome as the child achieves 'reversible thinking' (a vague phrase covering much ambiguity). Once we abandon the Piagetian viewpoint there is no particular reason to think that the development of ability to communicate is closely bound up with understanding the world.

Let us look first at the development of communication skills. While Piagetian psychology has seldom been applied in an unadulterated form to these, it tends in the direction of saying that we should emphasise having young children talk a lot among themselves so as to develop the ability to handle different viewpoints. Once this general skill in communication is mastered more detailed skills will naturally follow. Another version of this idea is involved in one of the uses that has been made of Goodman's theory of the reading process.

According to this approach when children read it is all-important that they pay attention to the meaning of the story or overall content of the passage and of virtually no importance that they recognise words or syllables. I have even heard it satirically alleged that some reading experts think you can read with your eyes closed! This rather aptly points up the problem that unless a child can quite rapidly recognise the first few words in a sentence they will have no chance of bringing any knowledge about the overall meaning of the text to bear on later words and phrases and that such guesses about the author's likely train of thought need to be supplemented with continual recognition of words to find out what the author is actually saying.

Both the Piagetian view and this false application of Goodman's ideas see communication in largely 'broad sweep' intellectual terms. If the child can master the overall plan behind the message then they will be able to send it (writing) or receive it (reading).

There is, however, nothing logically necessary about this view. If you want to send or receive a message then you may fail at any level from the lowest (e.g. recognising or spelling individual words) right up to the highest (understanding or planning the overall structure or gist of the message). We must therefore find out in each case of a child failing at reading or writing as to where the difficulty lies. Furthermore there are reasons for thinking that in these areas initial difficulties are more often found at the lower end of the scale (word recognition, spelling) than at the higher end (overall meaning). For one thing most children come to school having had four years of intensive practice at planning and understanding the overall structure of messages in speaking and listening. Yet these same children often have difficulty in reading and writing sentences and passages they could easily take in when listening and produce when speaking. This is an indication that their initial difficulties lie in mastering the mechanics of word recognition/spelling rather than in the area of overall meaning. More detailed research evidence reviewed later also supports this point of view. This does not, of course, mean that we should not try to make reading and writing into activities that involve overall meaning right from the start. By doing this we can help children acquire the motivation to practise lower-level skills. That however, means a very different orientation to teaching communication, particularly in the initial stages, from that implied by the idea that difficulties usually lie at the level of overall meaning.

We can now turn to teaching about maths and science. In this area Piagetian theory has been widely applied, chiefly via the recommendation to teach by having children act on the world, using apparatus of various kinds to make discoveries. At this very general level there is little to be said against such a strategy, provided that we remember that skills like doing sums on paper or using a calculating machine can and should substantially amplify the intuitions about the world that children derive from direct observation and discovery. It is a mistake to think that just because one understands the basic principles of arithmetic one will be a good calculator, just as it is a mistake to think that one who understands the basic principles of algebra will automatically be good at manipulating algebraic expressions. Adult mathematicians rarely revert to first principles when manipulating expressions or doing arithmetic; it simply takes too long to be forever reinventing techniques you should already know or to be interminably rediscovering facts about numbers that you could call up much more quickly from memory.

In reading and writing many of the relevant higher-order conceptual skills necessary to make progress have already emerged at age 5 and will continue to improve naturally as a part of the child's daily social interaction. In mathematics and science few of the higher-order concepts are present at age 5 and even at age 9 or 10 many children lack some of the concepts necessary to provide a rationale for the simple arithmetical computations that most Western schooling systems expect them to master. Thus improving higher-order conceptual skills is something that primary teachers should, and usually do, spend much more time on in the maths/science area.

In implementing primary science programmes Karplus and his associates in the United States have recommended the adoption of a 'learning cycle' consisting of the three phases 'exploration', 'concept introduction' and 'concept application'.[8] Thus 'exploration' might consist of a session where children are asked to investigate some phenomenon (e.g. weight of objects or types of flowers) using various measuring devices (if necessary) and some specimens they have collected. Hopefully this initial phase will stimulate interest and allow some conjectures to form in the child's mind. During 'concept introduction' a film or demonstration is shown in which say the concept of weight or a simple way of classifying flowers is explained. Finally during 'concept application' the children are given a session in which they actually apply the concept or method to do something, such as measuring weights or classifying some flowers. While it would be wrong to apply this learning cycle too rigidly it provides a good example of the application of learning theory in practice. While some commentators have seen Piagetian influences in the Karplus cycle, it is, like other activity methods, just as easily understood in terms of the hypothesis evaluation view of learning. In such cases we speed up the student's natural process of hypothesis formation by suggesting more general and valid principles than those that immediately present themselves to the learner.

The kind of concepts we have dealt with so far have included chiefly the rules and principles of science and mathematics. It is also useful to ask how children learn the problem solving strategies and mental models used in these areas.

One source that probably contributes a lot to strategy learning is simply success rate. If a certain way of attacking a problem has been successful in the past children will choose it again in the future. Seeing analogies between a familiar situation and an unknown one is also an important source of successful lines of attack. A further source of strategies is obviously instruction; someone tells you the best way to approach a problem.

Examples of these kinds of learning would be as follows. A child learns by experience that a good strategy to draw a human figure is to begin with the head or that a good strategy in dealing with a sum where there are multiples of 25 (such as $175 + 50$) is to remember that four twenty fives are a hundred. Alternatively the child may have learned these things by watching other people or by being told.

Everyone knows that learning to solve mathematical problems, do crossword puzzles or play chess is made much easier if, instead of just jumping into the activity and relying on native wit we try out a few problems (or a few games or puzzles) and then look at a book that gives instruction in strategy. Once again Karplus's learning cycle is relevant here: exploration without instruction, followed by an enunciation of principles, followed by activities where the principles can be applied.

Finally we can turn to learning mental models (sometimes called schemas). These are mental pictures that children use to help them understand the world as when they picture an atom as like a tiny pea or the water transport system of a plant as like the veins on the back of their hand. Here things are rather different. The learner may gradually receive assorted pieces of information about a topic like a town or a sea voyage by visits to different places in the town or reading about voyages of exploration in a book. Gradually these are organised into an overall 'picture' (e.g. a mental map of the town or a mental picture of routes taken by the explorers). As these two examples illustrate, the items of information may come from direct experience or from reading or other ways of being told information. A second style of learning involves helping the learner to form an overall picture by presenting a verbal or pictorial summary at the start of or during more detailed presentation of information or specific experiences. Ausubel *et al.* (1978) argue that such 'organisers' of knowledge should generally precede instruction and a number of studies have reported that this is more successful than learning without organisers or learning when organisers are presented at the end of instruction. When a picture such as a map or diagram is used as an organiser it is usual to either keep the picture up during the whole presentation or to keep bringing it out at various points during the session.[9]

Another useful general principle is that schemas are more readily learned when they are actively used to direct practical activities and problem solving. Such active use of the schema may take several forms. The first is simply its use to recall information from memory. Thus having formed a mental picture of voyages of discovery we might ask children to redescribe the voyages in their own words. A second use would be to set problems that require information that can be derived from the schema. Here we might ask the children to say what kinds of food they think the explorers could obtain in the places at which they called or how long each leg of the voyage took. A third way of manipulating the schema is rather more literal. Here we actually have children build a physical model of the schema, take one to pieces or redesign one that is made in modules. Examples of this are Dienes's blocks apparatus, unifix blocks, building a model of a pond, building a model of a spaceship and Leggo models. In the case of Dienes's blocks one cube represents a unit, a line of ten cubes (a 'long') represents 10, and a flat arrangement of 100 cubes represents 100. These actual models are intended to encourage the formation of a mental model of units, tens and hundreds. With unifix blocks children can put together and take apart the tens and hundreds, thus encouraging a thorough understanding of how the hundreds, tens and units all relate to one another. Likewise, building a model of a pond or spaceship will encourage the formation of a mental model of these things.

CONCLUSIONS

Piaget's descriptions of 'concrete operations' and 'formal operations' thinking are still of use for teachers provided we realise that development is not as neatly organised into stages as Piaget believed. On the other hand, his claim that development proceeds with sudden transitions between stages has been progressively eroded by more recent work.

There are two kinds of learning hierarchy: expression hierarchies used to express ideas and feelings; and logical hierarchies which structure the logical sequence of curriculum content. It has been common to counterpose the 'top-down' view of learning expression hierarchies of Piaget with the 'bottom-up' view of the construction of such hierarchies developed by Gagné. More recent thinking tends to emphasise that learning needs to concentrate on that level in the skill hierarchy that has been left the weakest by the child's previous experiences in a particular area. Thus it may be that for some students and topics more attention needs to be paid to high-level general concepts and principles, for others the problem may lie in the 'nitty gritty' difficulties at the bottom of the hierarchy. The ordering imposed on the curriculum by the logical sequence of concepts is now believed to be of crucial importance in determining the sequence of instruction.

Piaget's view that 'real understanding' develops chiefly through practical activity, especially in the primary years, has given way to a more eclectic view of learning that emphasises a combination of practical activities, observation and instruction as the best route to effective learning.

FURTHER READING

On the deficiencies of Piaget's logic and his explanations of stages see Seltman and Seltman (1985). For alternative proposals about the development of logical competence see Ennis (1976), Sternberg (1979), Langford (1981), Siegler (1981). On associationist views of learning see Wilson (1980); on hypothesis evaluation in children see Ault (1977), Whiteley (1985). Expositions of Gagné's ideas and extensions of them appear in Gagné (1984), Fischer (1980) and Fischer and Pipp (1984). A convenient introduction to Ausubel is Ausubel *et al.* (1978). A useful survey of Piaget's ideas is still Piaget and Inhelder (1969). There are innumerable books explaining Piaget to the teacher, any of which can be helpful.

NOTES

1. See Bennett (1977).
2. See later chapters for details.
3. See Osherson (1974), Ennis (1976), Sternberg (1979), Langford (1981), Siegler (1981).

4. See 3 and Bullock *et al.* (1982), Bullock (1985).
5. See, on Pascual-Leone, Trabasso and Foellinger (1978), Trabasso (1978), Kennedy (1983); on Halford and Wilson, Langford (1980, 1984); similar difficulties arise with the Case model. On the difficulty of equating short term memory with working memory see Brainerd and Kingma (1985).
6. The main exception to this is that on simplified tasks young children can be taught hypothesis testing in the laboratory (Spiker and Cantor, 1983); but it is doubtful that this occurs much in everyday life.
7. See Inhelder and Piaget (1955).
8. See Karplus (1980), pp. 161-9, Abraham and Renner (1986). Another approach to learning is that of Tennyson *et al.* (1981), McKinney *et al.* (1983) and Dunn (1983) which argues that presentation of a clear prototype (ideal example) is superior to either discovery or verbal explanation alone. It is unfortunate that they don't compare prototypes with discovery plus explanation, but the prototype method undoubtedly has its uses. Prototype learning should be clearly distinguished from schematic learning, something Norman (1980) fails to do.
9. For reviews see Lott (1983), Anderson and Armbruster (1984).

Chapter 2

READING

THE READING PROCESS AND LEARNING TO READ

I have already mentioned in the introduction that two rather divergent views of how children learn to read are popular at present; that which sees the problem faced by children as primarily one of understanding the overall meaning of the text and that which sees the problem as primarily one of learning to recognise words and syllables fluently.

To understand the points at issue here it is necessary to understand something about how adults read as it is these skills the child is aiming to master. Goodman (1967, 1968, 1970) has proposed a model of the adult reading process that is now very widely accepted and will be adopted as the basis of my discussion here. We can best approach this model by thinking of a very naive view of reading. According to this naive view when we read a sentence like 'The dog chased the cat' we first of all look at the first word, recognise this as 'the', then look at the second word, recognise this as 'dog' and so on. Once we have read the whole sentence we then try to work out its syntax and having worked out the syntax we work out the meaning. We see that 'The dog' is the subject of the sentence, 'chased' is the main verb and 'the cat' is the object. Putting this together with the meaning of the words we see that the dog was affecting the cat by chasing it.

Goodman pointed out that there are a number of reasons for thinking that this process is not neatly sequential in the way outlined here. Instead of reading off all the words in a sentence before working out its syntax and meaning what we actually do is to start working out the syntax and meaning as we go along. We then use these partially formed guesses about what the syntax and meaning are to predict ahead the words we are about to encounter. This process of guessing ahead is so important that we actually skip some words and we only look very briefly at others to make sure that casual inspection is consistent with our predictions. Try for instance reading the following sentence: 'It was a cold day and Jill was glad to be able to buy a nice cup of hot lea.' If you were not alerted and found this in the middle of a passage of prose you would be likely to read 'lea' as 'tea'; 'lea' is the right general shape and thus confirms the expectation generated by the stock phrase 'a nice hot cup of . . .' You would be less likely to read the phrase 'a nice hot cup of elephant' as 'a nice hot cup of tea' because 'elephant' is too long and the wrong shape. In general we also read the actual letters more closely at the beginning of a passage or when the passage is about a novel topic or contains a lot of novel information.

We can see how children are reading more easily than how adults are reading because children make more mistakes. A child might read the sentence 'I ate some ice cream' and say 'I ate some ice dream'. Here Goodman would say that the child has used the cues provided by the look of the word ('graphophonic cues'), has possibly also used the information provided by the syntax (the word is a noun) but has almost certainly not used the information provided by the meaning of the sentence, as we don't eat 'ice dreams' (except in a very fanciful sense). On the other hand, a child who reads out 'I ate some ice cubes' would be paying attention to the meaning of the sentence as we do eat ice cubes.

There is no doubt that some children tend to read by relying mainly on the appearance of the words, while others rely more on meaning. It should be emphasised, however, that those who rely on meaning also rely heavily on the look of the words and on syntax; they need to look at words carefully at the beginning of a passage and of each sentence to find out what is likely to follow. There is also not much doubt that children who rely solely on the look of the words tend to be poor readers. Many of them are those children who frown painfully as they tackle each new word, spending a long time working it out. By the time they have puzzled out a new word they have often forgotten the preceding ones. There are a few children who read more fluently but only read the actual words, but this is less usual.

The disputed issue is this. Do poor readers tend to rely on the look of each word as it comes up because they fail to realise that they should think about the meaning, or do they fail to think about the meaning because they have such difficulty in recognising the individual words that they tend to lose sight of the overall message? Our answer to this question will have considerable influence on the way we teach. If we think the problem is that such children don't know they should look at the meaning then remediating the problem will be relatively easy so long as right from the outset we encourage children to read for meaning.[1] One way this has been done is by the 'language experience' method of having the child make up a sentence. The teacher then writes down the sentence and that becomes part of the child's reading material, thus ensuring the child knows that the object of reading is to obtain meaning.

My main argument against the theory just outlined is that in Anglo-Saxon countries many schools have over the past ten years adopted language experience methods and other ways of emphasising reading for meaning. Those schools have not been able to report any dramatic improvement in reading achievement. Many teachers have, on the contrary, felt obliged to supplement language experience methods with activities like reading packs of flash cards derived from cutting up the child-generated sentences in order to improve word recognition skills.[2]

These doubts are reinforced by research findings. The majority of studies have not confirmed the notion that proficient readers use context cues more than less proficient readers. Evidence is more divided as to whether less proficient readers use graphophonic cues more than proficient readers (Harding *et al.*, 1985). On the other hand, size of sight vocabulary (words immediately recognised without sounding-out) varies strongly and directly with reading proficiency (Adams and Huggins, 1985).

In addition, Woodford and Fowler (1983, 1984) summarise a number of studies showing that poor readers differ from good readers in their diminished ability to use the graphic (written appearance) and phonetic (sound) aspects of words, though they are as good as fluent readers in dealing with word meaning. Freebody and Tirre (1985) found that low ability students benefited more from an initial reading programme directed at word recognition skills, high ability students more from the language experience approach.

This leads us to consider the alternative view that failing to read for meaning is usually a product of poor word and syllable recognition skills (see Lesgold and Perfetti, 1978).[3] If this is the case then we need to pay considerable attention to the development of these skills. This can be done in two ways. One is, as in the example of the flash cards just mentioned, to actually take recognition skills out of the context of the normal reading process and drill them. The other is just to rely on more reading of whole sentences and texts. These issues lie beyond the scope of this coverage, but common experience suggests that both methods as well as some explicit instruction about how to pay attention to the shapes of letters and words is advisable.[4]

CONCEPTIONS OF STORY

In the previous section we considered the idea that a major difficulty that children face in learning to read is that they don't understand they are supposed to read for meaning. In this section we will deal with the related idea that children face difficulty in learning to read not because they don't know they are to read for meaning but because the structural organisation of the stories they read eludes them.

One initial reason for thinking that this theory of learning to read is also at fault is that research on children's understanding of the story line of a story shows that this is usually well enough developed by 8 or 9 years to allow children to follow a simple story, whereas a substantial minority of children are still experiencing difficulty in reading simple stories at this age. An informal demonstration of this point can be found in the fact that many poor readers are great television watchers. The television allows them to go straight to the meaning of a story through something they can recognise, namely pictures. Their problems begin when they try to reach the meaning of a story through something they find hard to recognise, namely words.

The first theoretical issue that confronts us in looking at story structure is whether children and adults absorb a standard story structure that exists 'in' the story or whether each constructs their own version of story structure depending upon preconceptions, situation and interests. In his classic book *Remembering* Bartlett (1932) approached finding the meaning of stories as a constructive 'effort after meaning'. Memory for stories involved attempting to reconstruct the story from this constructed 'schema' along with 'corrections' supplied by images and sensational or incongruous detail. The view that story structure is not constructed but rather exists objectively 'in' the text has been more popular since Bartlett's day.[5] The constructive view has, however, made a comeback in recent years, both within general linguistic and cognitive theory and in the study of children's conceptions of story.[6]

The following reasons for this shift of emphasis can be given. Both Dooling and Lachman (1972) and Bransford and Johnson (1972) provided formal verification for the rather obvious fact that stories that don't seem to make sense without certain background information do make perfect sense with it. A related point is that without such information readers may well invent it in different ways. A piece about Tom Thumb, for instance, might not begin by informing the reader that he was very small. On learning that Tom Thumb rode inside a horse's ear the reader would have two possibilities; to imagine that Tom Thumb was very small or that the horse was very large. A further reason is that Bartlett (1932) discovered, and later researchers have verified, that when stories are recalled certain additional facts are included that were not stated in the original but that may be inferred from it.[7]

A second theoretical issue relates to the form of rules used in describing story structure. The most popular assumption here is that the rules generate a hierarchical structure, similar in form to Chomsky's (1965) base structure syntax.[8] To give an example of this, Mandler and Johnson (1977) took Bartlett's story 'War of the Ghosts' and decomposed it into six episodes. Of these episodes 1, 2, 5 and 6 were held to be the major episodes, while episodes 3 and 4 were described as sub-parts of episode 2. Thus the whole story was divided into four main episodes, the second one being divided into three smaller parts. The event structure of the story was described as a hierarchy of major and minor events. In addition to the hierarchical 'base' rules Mandler and Johnson (1977) and Johnson and Mandler (1980) also suggest a 'transformational component' in story structure that maps these base structures into sometimes convoluted surface forms.

The biggest problem of such models, as admitted by Johnson and Mandler (1980, p.83), is that elements that may be psychologically important to the person understanding the story can appear low down in the hierarchy of episodes. This is partly because while an event may be part of a larger episode its importance may be disproportionate to the amount of time it takes. Even in terms of time taken to complete it, a subordinate episode might be much longer than one high in the hierarchy.

A major argument against hierarchical theories of story structure is that they do not appear to represent 'gist' as key events are not distinguished from detail. Another question that has to be asked is why structure should be assumed to be hierarchical rather than taking some other form. A non-hierarchical view that has considerable promise is that of Kintsch and van Dijk (1978). This represents story structure as a network of relations uniting the various propositions contained in the story. In a hierarchical theory, each element is only related to those directly above it in the hierarchy. In Kintsch and van Dijk's model an element may relate to as many other elements as it is found to have some relation with. The relation these authors concentrate upon is that found when two propositions involve the same person or thing (they call this the argument) (p.386). Presumably other relations could be considered. The sum of such relations is called a 'coherence graph'. In addition Kintsch and van Dijk (1978) describe the 'macrostructure' of a text as a set of 'macropropositions' that are used to summarise other propositions. Presumably various kinds of coherence graph could be used to represent the structure of such macropropositions.[9]

A third major theoretical issue is whether purely formal studies of story grammar are adequate or whether analysis should concentrate primarily on content, as do Kintsch and van Dijk (1978). Black and Wilensky (1979) provide an extensive critique of the purely formal approach and advocate concentration upon content.

We turn now to the various means by which children's understanding of story concepts can be assessed. These may be listed as involving immediate comprehension, recognition of aspects of the story after time has elapsed, recall of the story and the analysis of stories made up by the child. Before proceeding to examine each of these areas in detail, a number of studies that have combined several means of assessment should be mentioned.

Waters and Lomenick (1983) asked children to tell a story based on a prompt word, such as 'winter' or 'a farm'. They then recalled this after two weeks. In another experiment children listened to passages generated in this way and were then asked to recall them after two weeks. It was found that the amount of organisation in the generated stories and the percentage of the passage recalled increased with age from 8 years to college age. This increase in recall was, however, gradual rather than stage-like, in the case of self-generated stories increasing from 30 per cent-51 per cent and in the case of stories generated by others from 27 per cent-41 per cent.

Brown (1975) compared children's recognition, reconstruction and recall of stories. Stories were presented accompanied by pictures of the objects and characters in the story. In recognition, the child had to recognise the picture sequence from other sequences; in reconstruction to construct it by assembling pictures and ordering them; in recall to tell it orally. The study focused on the order of events, which 7 year olds were able to recall and reconstruct equally well. Five and 6 year old children were found to have considerable difficulty in retelling the story events in the right order, though they could reconstruct and recognise the correct order. Both Fraisse (1963) and Piaget (1969) had believed that the inability of young children to recount events in their correct order was due to lack of appropriate concepts with which to organise experience. Brown's study showed that the problem lies in the child's immature expository powers rather than in poor conceptual abilities.

In view of Brown's (1975) findings it will be advisable to look first at studies of children's comprehension of stories, which should give us the best estimate of a child's likely abilities when confronted with the task of reading. The most complete study in this area to date appears to be that of Whaley (1981). This is of additional interest in that he studied children's reactions to reading as opposed to listening to stories. Children read three stories and were either asked to predict what would happen next after the text finished or to fill in a missing episode. The structural adequacy of these additions was checked against expectations derived from Johnson and Mandler's (1980) story grammar. It was found that 8 year olds employed structural expectations less often than 11 or 18 year olds, but that readers at all ages had qualitatively similar structural expectations.[10]

A significant study that focused on recognition of story content was Prawat, Cancelli and Cook (1976), who found that even 5 year olds tended to recognise true inferences from a passage, but were less adept at distinguishing explicitly stated and inferred information than older children. Koblinski and Cruse (1981) found using recognition techniques that presenting material to assist in schema formation had a greater impact upon 10 year olds when presented prior to reading a passage than when presented afterwards, indicating that such material affects the initial encoding of material in memory more than its retrieval from memory.[11]

Finally there have been a number of studies of children's recall of stories. As these are less directly relevant to assessing the understanding of story structure nothing will be said about them here beyond the well-established point that recall is considerably harder than recognition or reconstruction.[12] Ability to tell stories also lags behind ability to understand them.[13]

In conclusion, Fraisse (1963) and Piaget (1969) thought that young children retell stories with events in a jumbled order because they do not understand story structure or concepts of temporal ordering. More recent studies, particularly that of Brown (1975), have shown that asking children to recall stories is a poor way to test understanding of the story as it imposes the additional difficulty of recalling and restructuring the information given. When tested by recognition and reconstruction methods children have been found to understand considerably more about story structure than believed by Fraisse (1963) and Piaget (1969). This calls into question the view that a major obstacle to children's learning to read is their lack of understanding of story structure. Reinforcing this conclusion, Weaver and Dickinson (1982) and McConaughy (1985) found that poor readers between 9 and 15 years were just as good at recalling story structure as normal readers.[14]

CONCEPTS OF PRINT

The major issues here arise in deciding how children's conscious and verbally expressed understanding of print and the activity of reading relate to the ability to actually read.[15] In order to be able to read children must know about two things: the functions and purposes served by reading and the way in which marks on the paper represent language that is originally for the child something to hear and speak. Most children eventually come to know that they can read for entertainment, for information, for escape, for examinations. They also come to know that English is written from left to right and from the top to the bottom of the page, that sentences are made of words, words of letters, that we begin a sentence with a capital letter and end with a full stop. These and other similar pieces of information are called 'concepts of print'.

The question arises: what role do these play in learning to read? There are reasons for thinking that children's earliest understanding is usually of a non-verbal variety and young children often have great difficulty in putting what they know into words. When we consider that most adults would find it hard to put into words how to tie a shoelace or how to ride a bicycle, we should beware of thinking that children can explain in words everything they know how to do. This reflection is particularly important in approaching the topic of concepts of print as the idea has become popular that a conscious, verbally-expressed understanding of what print is forms a necessary preliminary to learning to read and that failure to learn to read is often caused by lack of conscious understanding of what reading is.[16]

As this idea is inherently rather implausible, it is worth looking at the evidence its authors use to support it. The initial stimulus came from the observation that 5 year olds are often unable to explain what reading is for or how its coding system works when asked. To jump from this to conclude either that they have no intuitive knowledge of reading or that this is what is holding up their reading development is of course invalid. More recent research also shows that 5 year olds normally know a lot more about print than originally claimed (Hiebert, 1981).

Another line of research has tried to show that tests of verbally expressed knowledge of print correlate with reading achievement, a finding reported by Johns (1980), who correlated Clay's (1972a) *Concepts About Print Test* with reading achievement. Johns rightly warns the reader that this does not establish that knowledge of concepts of print causes good reading achievement: 'Have above-average readers' concepts of print caused them to be good readers or are their concepts about print a result of their reading ability?' At present he rightly concludes that we don't really know.

More plausible analyses of the relation of concepts of print to reading achievement have been advanced by Ehri (1979) and Hiebert (1980), for both of whom reading ability is partly cause and partly effect of an understanding of concepts of print. Hiebert (1980) also found that among preschoolers the only measure of home environment to correlate significantly with an aspect of print awareness was the mother's attitude to teaching the child, which correlated with the child's ability to name letters. Hiebert comments that this may reflect the circumstance that at present letter naming is often the only aspect of print awareness that parents teach children and that if parents had a wider understanding of print awareness they might be able to teach concepts of more use in the actual reading process. It may be added that letter naming is an example of a print awareness concept that plays virtually no role in the actual reading process.

The most widely used methods of assessing children's understanding of print concepts have been Reid's (1958, 1966) and Downing's (1970) method of loosely structured interviews and Clay's (1972a) *Concepts About Print Test*. The former method tends to lean heavily in the direction of verbal explanation by the child. Clay's test involves a mixture of requests for verbal explanation and requests to demonstrate knowledge by action. An example of the former is that the child is shown a full stop or period and asked to name it or explain its function (item 16). An example of the latter is the child is asked to show by reference to a printed page which direction we read in (item 14). Unfortunately studies using this test have not clearly distinguished these two kinds of items, though they obviously tap different kinds of knowledge.[17] It is, however, of considerable interest that when Day and Day (1979a) factor-analysed results from this test they found four main factors: book orientation concepts; print-direction concepts; letter-work concepts; advanced print concepts. Of these the first and second groups of items were, with only one exception, action-knowledge items, while items in the third all involved verbal explanation. The fourth was a mixture of the two types of knowledge. The methods of assessing print concepts published by Agnew (1982) and Downing (1970) also involve such a mixture. It would mark a significant advance in this area for researchers to distinguish more clearly between action knowledge and verbal knowledge and to try to separate out more clearly those aspects of print understanding that are likely to contribute directly to the reading process (such as sounding out letters) and those that are not (such as naming letters). It would also mark a considerable advance if it could be shown that instruction in concepts of print improves later reading achievement. Mayfield (1983) has reported a successful study in which children were taught concepts of print in Canadian kindergarten grades, but the later impact of such experiences on reading have yet to be assessed.

READING STRATEGIES

Chall (1979) has argued that in the early stages of learning to read the problem is largely that of decoding symbols and then relating what has been decoded to an already developed ability to follow a storyline. Around the fourth or fifth grade the aim of reading changes from that of practising skills to that of gaining new knowledge and information, particularly from textbooks. 'Learning to read' is replaced by 'reading to learn'.

In this new phase of reading it is preferable for the reader to begin using some of the methods of the skilled reader: to scan headings and chapter titles to find out the overall topic; to locate passages likely to answer particular questions from the contents or index; to skip read; to read actively with an effort to isolate the main points or gist.

One method of promoting active reading in the upper primary years has been evaluated empirically. This is called Directed Reading and Thinking Activity (DRTA) (Stauffer, 1975). This is divided into a number of steps that students proceed through in approaching a passage. The first is to read the title and the first paragraph, look at the pictures if any and predict what the passage is about. In the reading stage students read the passage to see if their predictions are right. In the final 'proving' stage they are asked to give reasons (out loud or on paper) as to why their predictions were right or wrong. Evaluations show that this method improves comprehension and recall of passages (Cook and Mayer, 1983).

A number of other methods of encouraging student activity while reading have been widely used and evaluated with secondary and college students, particularly note taking, summarising, underlining significant sentences and answering questions on the passage. Studies show these methods tend to be more effective when implemented actively by the student making the notes or summary than when notes and summary are provided. Questions on the other hand are effective even when set by others provided they relate to issues likely to arouse the student's interest (Cook and Mayer, 1983). The effectiveness of some of these methods has been positively evaluated for the upper primary grades (Scardamalia and Bereiter, 1984). Surprisingly, the effects of group discussion of passages by students have received little evaluation, though this too provides a useful method of encouraging active reading.

CONCLUSIONS

It is time to focus attention on issues that are of most direct relevance to the classroom teacher. The most important of such issues seem to be as follows. Is it worth trying to teach children how to read for meaning, concepts of story or concepts of print? If so, how much time should be devoted to these things in relation to other aspects of reading? The answer to the first question must be cautiously in the affirmative, given certain qualifications already discussed. It is the second question that is so vital for the classroom teacher and is, unfortunately, too little asked or answered. Specialists working in the above mentioned areas have too often fallen victim to that tendency, common in specialists, to think that if their area was attended to, reading problems would dramatically lessen. There is, however, little evidence to support such claims. The fact that children on entry to school are unsure of the generalised purposes or the nature of the coding systems involved in reading does not show that those children who reach the fourth or fifth year of schooling and remain very weak readers do so for this reason.

We can achieve more insight into the problem of learning to read by returning to the first principles of mature reading enunciated by Goodman (1967, 1970). Mature readers use their knowledge of graphophonic cues (the shapes of letters and words), syntax and meaning, including story structure. Commonsense would, however, suggest that the point at which the beginning reader is weakest is in graphophonic cues. Children come to school with sufficient grasp of the syntax and meaning system of their native language to approach most early texts that are not wilfully divorced from the everyday life of the child. The most common cause of 'reading the words', particularly of laboriously trying to sound out each individual letter, is a poor ability to recognise words or phrases as wholes. Only by building up a reasonably large 'sight vocabulary', that is words or phrases recognised immediately as wholes, can the beginning reader begin to read quickly. It is only by reading quickly that children can keep the story line going in their head. While some children may be slowed down by the belief that every word has to be read correctly, even when they have got over this and are trying to read for meaning, they will never do so without a sizeable sight vocabulary. This is not to say that the phonic skills necessary to attack unfamiliar words are without use, but unless accompanied by sight vocabulary they will never lead to fluent reading. This general analysis of learning to read is supported by studies showing that the level of oral language proficiency of beginning readers has only a moderate correlation with success in learning to read.[18] Wells (1978) suggests that it is only children with rather unusually slow language development who are hindered by poor 'oracy', that is poor syntax and poor ability to grasp stories.

The upshot of these considerations is to suggest that while for occasional children problems connected with poor syntax, story understanding or concepts of print may be the particular block in their ability to progress in reading, for the majority of children the biggest initial hurdle is sight vocabulary and initial instruction should aim to make sure that plenty of time is devoted to developing this. It is this and the development of a positive attitude to reading that are the issues requiring most attention during initial reading. As reading progresses students should be encouraged to read actively, to pose questions and construct schematic meaning for the passage as a whole.

FURTHER READING

The two classic articles on the interactionist view of reading adopted here are Lesgold and Perfetti (1978) and Perfetti and Lesgold (1979); read either, not both. Briggs *et al.* (1985), Beech (1985) and Bryant and Bradley (1985) give up to date presentations of this view. Chall's (1979) article is also recommended. Anyone interested in recent work on story structure should look at Stein and Glenn (1982), Stein (1982) and Trabasso *et al.* (1984). On the development of concepts of print see Ehri (1979) and Hiebert (1980). An excellent review on promoting reading strategies is given by Cook and Mayer (1983).

NOTES

1. For expositions of this approach see Paris and Lindauer (1982), Kennedy (1984), Tunmer and Bowey (1983), Canney and Winograd (1979), Spiro and Myers (1979). Donaldson (1978, Chs. 7, 8) leans in this direction with some qualifications.
2. Francis (1982, Ch. 7) points out that there may be a small minority of children who do not know the purposes of reading at the beginning of school.

3. See also Morrison (1984), Simpson *et al.* (1983), Perfetti and Lesgold (1979), Bryant and Bradley (1985), Beech (1985).
4. There is also considerable evidence that children differ widely in their approach to word recognition, some relying on letters, others on overall shape (Treiman, 1984). Harding *et al.* (1985) found that reliance on whole word recognition also increases with age.
5. Sachs (1967), Stein and Glenn (1979), Johnson and Mandler (1980).
6. Bransford *et al.* (1972), Dooling and Lachman (1972), Bransford and Johnson (1972), Lakoff (1971), Van Dijk (1973), Spiro (1980), Goetz and Armbruster (1980).
7. See Prawatt *et al.* (1976).
8. Rummelhart (1975), Botvin and Sutton-Smith (1977), Stein and Glenn (1979), Mandler and Johnson (1977), Johnson and Mandler (1980), Black and Bower (1980), Stein and Trabasso (1982).
9. A discussion of some limitations of network theory is given in Johnson-Laird *et al.* (1984). A third approach, not treated here, is Nelson's 'script' theory (McCartney and Nelson, 1981; Slackman and Nelson, 1984; Hudson and Nelson, 1983). The main difficulty of this approach is that it has problems in explaining how unfamiliar and novel plots are understood. A fourth approach, only recently developed, is the 'goal structure' view of Stein and Trabasso (1984), Stein (1982) and Trabasso *et al.* (1984).
10. See also Pearson *et al.* (1979), Paris and Lindauer (1976), Paris and Upton (1976), Markman (1977, 1979, 1981), Townsend (1983).
11. On summarising texts see Brown and Day (1983), Brown *et al.* (1978), Brown and Smiley (1978). Of related interest is Fayol (1978).
12. On story recall see also Stein and Glenn (1977, 1979), Nezworski *et al.* (1982), Hoppe-Graff *et al.* (1980), Glenn (1980). On children's rating of the importance of story elements see Hoppe-Graff and Scholer (1980), Brown and Smiley (1977) and Denhiere and Le Ny (1980).
13. On story production and the cultural universality of the structure of folk tales see Botvin and Sutton-Smith (1977), Propp (1968), Johnson and Mandler (1980), Kintsch (1977), Kintsch and Greene (1978), Mandler and Johnson (1980). On the cultural universality of stages in cognitive development see Dasen (1975, 1977, 1980).
14. It is true that Oakhill (1984) found inferences about stories superior in good readers, but Weaver and Dickinson's poor readers had mainly specific reading disability, while in Oakhill's study reading ability may have been confounded with general ability.
15. On this issue in relation to metalinguistic awareness see Brown (1978, 1980), Clark (1978) and Van Kleek (1982). On metalinguistic awareness more generally see Weir (1962), Gleitman et al (1972),

Smith (1973), Spielberger (1965), Bellefroid and Ferreiro (1979), Van Kleek (1982), Templeton and Spivey (1980), Morris (1980), Liberman *et al.* (1974), Huttenlocher (1964), Holden and McGintie (1972), Ehri (1975), Liberman (1973), Zhurova (1973), Read (1973), Hakes (1980), Gleitman *et al.* (1972), James and Miller (1973), Bohannon (1975), Scholl and Ryan (1975), Ryan (1980), Boutet *et al.* (1983), Markman (1977), Robinson and Robinson (1976a,b, 1977), Paterson and Kister (1981), Robinson (1981a,b), Robinson and Robinson (1980, 1982, 1983), Osherson and Markman (1975), Berthoud (1978, 1980), Tunmer and Herriman (1983).

16. Reid (1958, 1966, 1983), Mattingley (1972, 1978, 1979), Downing (1979).
17. Clay (1972b,c), Zinck (1978), Day and Day (1979a,b), Johns (1980).
18. Francis (1974), Wells (1978). Reid and Hresko (1980) report, as we might expect, considerably higher correlations among learning disabled children.

Chapter 3

WRITING

THE WRITING PROCESS AND LEARNING TO WRITE

In the chapter on reading I argued against placing too much faith in the idea that initial learning difficulties usually lie in failures of strategic organisation. In dealing with writing things are a little different. Instead of taking most of their cues about strategic organisation from the text, the writer has to make up strategic organisation and has to code up the message in a fashion that is appropriate for its intended audience. These things do make for difficulties in writing and most teachers who deal with writing beyond the very first stages find that children take a long time to learn about these things. Indeed, few of us ever stop learning about them.

In some other respects there are parallels between the areas of reading and writing. It is unlikely, in my view, that many children fail in writing because they don't know the general purposes or functions of writing. It is also the case that progress is often impeded, particularly in the early stages, by the lack of low level skills, especially spelling.[1] In addition, children who spend a long time thinking of a spelling (either a standard spelling or an invented one), tend to lose track of what they are doing in the way of overall organisation and coding for the audience.

How do these ideas relate to the most visible recent trend in teaching primary writing, process writing? There are various kinds of process writing approach, but as that of Graves (1975, 1983) has been most influential in the primary school I shall concentrate on that. The fundamental premise of all such approaches is that in the past we have allowed adults to write one way and children another. Adults are allowed to choose a topic, write rough drafts, play around with ideas, mull things over. Children were sat down, given a topic and asked to write something about it right away; when they got older they faced (as they still do) the 40 minute exam essay. In the Graves process writing approach we encourage children to behave like adults, to choose their own topic, to mull it over, write a first draft, come back and edit it. It is worth noting even at this point that this rationale, commonly given for process writing approaches, is already slightly fallacious. We don't always allow adults to choose their topics, write rough drafts or mull things over; think of being a journalist and writing an article your editor told you to get finished quickly or the minutes of a meeting or a letter to a government department. Furthermore, our tendency to wish to write rough drafts tends to depend on the familiarity and difficulty of the topic. Few people bother with rough drafts of personal letters, while many journalists write their stories out in one draft.

However, the Graves process writing approach goes much further than simply copying the adult composing process as seen in certain more demanding situations. It also advocates that children invent their own spelling, correct their own spelling and discuss one another's writing in 'conferences'. There is a minimum of teacher correction and only a modest amount of teacher suggestion, usually along the lines of 'Well, what do you think of this?', or 'Does this read smoothly here?'

One underlying reason that these more radical innovations work is that children are able to pick up knowledge about spelling from reading. As adults we often want to write a word down to see if we are spelling it right. When children re-read their writing they notice that 'it looks wrong' provided they have read the word fairly often when reading. For this reason it is most unlikely that the Graves writing approach will be successful unless children are doing a considerable amount of reading.

Having outlined the general features of the Graves approach it is time to focus on the more specific concept development questions raised at the outset of this section. I reiterate that it is unlikely that the Graves approach, or any other approach, will be primarily of benefit because it teaches children the functions and purposes of writing on a purely intellectual level. It is much more likely to be of benefit because it teaches them how to carry out functions like conveying feelings or information in a relatively pleasant way. At the same time the Graves process approach does allow children as they proceed to the upper grades of the primary school, to think at greater length about organisation and audience. I have, however, one considerable reservation here, particularly as regards the top two years of the primary school and right through secondary school. For both Graves and Elbow (an exponent of process writing for older students) explicitly prohibit teachers from using that old suggestion to students 'begin with a plan'.

In thinking about the use of plans in writing it is important to be flexible. Both adults and children are often more willing to begin with a plan in writing about something they are familiar with. In dealing with unfamiliar material they may prefer to write a first draft without a plan and then produce one for the second draft. However, once children leave the purely narrative, story-telling, stage of writing and begin to write descriptions or explanations or discussions, planning is essential and both common experience and general theory suggest that at some point in the composing process it is worth making the plan explicit by writing it down. This is certainly what most adult writers do when faced with difficult or unfamiliar topics.

THE DEVELOPMENT OF OVERALL ORGANISATION

Little (1975, 1978) has shown that the types of content organisation found in children's school writing develop roughly as follows: at 7 years, about 50 per cent is recording, reporting and generalised narrative, about 50 per cent is imaginative, expressive or interactive. Both such forms involve a mixture of organisation by time (X happened, then Y happened, then Z happened) and organisation by association of ideas, as in the following poetic description of a birthday party: 'Ice-creams are dancing in the circus. Pens are dancing in the air.' Here the ideas of dancing and of inanimate objects being happy are used to link sentences together. At 10 years, 50 per cent is still recording, reporting or narrative, while 25 per cent is now imaginative, expressive or interactive and 25 per cent consists of generalising and classifying, such as pieces dealing with types of cars or breeds of dogs. At 14 years the pattern remains much the same. It is not until 17 years that we find speculation and theorising forming about 25 per cent of scripts, largely at the expense of expressive and imaginative writing.

These shifts seem to reflect the changes in children's levels of thinking that occur as they grow older, but they do so with a considerable time delay. Classificatory thinking is well advanced in the child's general mental development by age 7 (Inhelder and Piaget, 1964), but does not show up in writing until age 10, on average. Theorising and the consideration of abstractions is well advanced in the child's general thinking by age 14 (Inhelder and Piaget, 1955), but does not appear in writing until 17 years.

Wilkinson *et al.* (1981) agreed with Little's general findings but produced a more refined system of classifying children's writing that takes into account levels of complexity and competence within broader categories. Their initial category of 'Describing' (similar to Little's 'recording, reporting') contains such simple levels as 'partial information' and 'recording'. In describing a game the child might write (as 'partial information') 'wene you get to near the red circle you would of de caught' (often get caught). This explains only one aspect of the game and concentrates on a description of what tends to happen rather than of the rules. On the other hand, only one-third of 7 year olds were able to rise to the level of 'reporting', the most advanced kind of 'Describing' in which there is a full chronological account given of how the game proceeds from beginning to end, as in this charming account of how to play 'Kerplunk': 'This is how you play Kerplunk first you get this tube with holes in and then you fix it to the tray and then you put the skinny sticks in the holes and as soon as all the skinny sticks are in the holes you put in the marbles on top of the skinny sticks then each player takes a stick in turn the way to go round is clockwise and the player to get the least marbles is the winner.'

This piece only rises to the level of 'Interpreting' (Little's 'generalising') at the end when the rule to determine who wins is explained; other rules are explained in terms of what happens. Explaining a single rule is the simplest level of 'Interpreting'. More complex forms of this category are 'inferring' and 'deducing'.

In their sample of 7-13 year olds Wilkinson *et al.* found no examples that produced a coherent deductive account of the rules of a game. Partial information declined from 69 per cent at 7 years, to 7 per cent at 13 years, while explanations of rules rose from 45 per cent at 7 years, to 93 per cent at 13 years.

Wilkinson *et al.* also asked for written comments on the topic 'Would it work if children came to school when they liked and did what they liked there?' At 7 years two-thirds of the children offered only 'partial information', while the remainder made some attempt at interpretation, usually the explanation that they would abolish school because it would be more enjoyable for them personally if they didn't have to go! By 10 years of age as many as 60 per cent were able to adopt a hypothesis (e.g. 'Children are to cease going to school') and then deduce from this various conclusions ('They won't learn anything so they won't get a job' being a common one). It seems likely that the widespread belief that children of primary age are unable to tackle hypothetical questions of the kind posed here has led to an under-estimation of their powers of written argument. Many of Wilkinson *et al.*'s 10 year olds not only gave quite extensive lists of consequences stemming from the hypothetical abolition of school, but were also able to correct their initial hypothesis if such deductions proved unfavourable to it. Thus the student might begin by assuming that school should not be compulsory, review the results that would follow from this and then decide that there should be an element of compulsion in schooling.

The material just described shows that by the top two forms of primary school the predominant use of the descriptive and story forms of writing is beginning to be replaced by classification and argument. As these appear, it is worth thinking of trying to make them more explicit. Thus in a piece dealing with types of cars it is worth pointing out that information about each type of car needs to be collected together into its own section. At second draft stage this may be done by encouraging a list of the types to be covered and the use of section headings. One study found that just asking children from 8-12 years to think about a plan for five minutes before beginning writing improved their planning.[2]

EGOCENTRISM, CODING AND AUDIENCES

It has often been suggested that the difficulties young children suffer in communication known as 'egocentrism' and 'coding problems' hinder their progress in writing. Piaget (1926) found that young children talk as though the person listening to them already knows things that in reality they do not. This is known as communicative egocentrism: the tendency of children to talk without reference to the needs of the listener. Flavell *et al.* (1968) found that particular difficulty arose, even in middle childhood, when several listeners were involved.

Piaget (1926), as in many of his studies, tends to rather overplay the disabilities of the young child in this area and other investigators have been concerned to emphasise their positive achievements. Thus, in talking to both the blind and infants, even 3 and 4 year olds will considerably modify their speech.[3] Menig-Peterson (1975) found that young children were able to modify their speech depending upon the presumed prior knowledge of the listener. Ackerman (1978) has also shown that children of 5 years old are able to make quite sophisticated inferences about a speaker's beliefs from what the speaker explicitly states.

A second stimulus that has been influential in this area has been the thesis of Bernstein (1965, 1971, 1981) that certain kinds of social environment encourage children to talk in a 'restricted code', that is in a way that is directed to the needs of a particular listener rather than to those of an unspecified listener. Thus in talking to its mother the child can assume all sorts of common understanding that becomes less relevant in dealing with teachers at school and even less relevant when faced with examiners.

Subsequent discussion and research on Bernstein's thesis have clarified a number of points. First of all it is not the case that the tendency for children to have this kind of difficulty is perfectly correlated with social class membership.[4] Second, while there is an association between 'restricted' speech and poor educational attainment, there is an even stronger one between indifferent attitudes to and poor knowledge of literacy in the home and educational attainment.[5] Thus while problems in assessing the audiences for communications may be one contributing cause of poor educational attainment it is probably not the only or even the main one. Both these problems are acknowledged by Bernstein (1981).

A third general line of research into children's understanding of audiences which has come into prominence in recent years relates to children's reactions to their own failure to communicate their meaning to other people. One aspect of this process is that children seem to become aware of ambiguity in messages more from the reactions of others than from their own experience of uncertainty when presented with such messages. Robinson (1981a) has also reviewed literature on the more general problem of how children learn to overcome their problems in communication. Younger children, around 5 years, still typically blame the listener for inadequate message comprehension, while by 7 years many children will blame the speaker (Robinson and Robinson, 1976a,b). However younger children, who are still listener blamers, still sometimes mention that the message was inadequate and they quite frequently put their own message into other words when faced with listener incomprehension.[6]

This leads us to consider what happens when the child's communications are misunderstood in everyday life. Robinson (1981a) reports a reanalysis of some recordings in homes, preschools and primary classrooms in Australia.[7] The chief findings were that inadequate messages were relatively rare, with children giving inadequate messages only 8 or 9 per cent of the time. Reactions to message failure ranged from requests for repetition and for more information to the giving of guesses or various alternative meanings by the listener. Explicit explanations of why communication had failed were rare except in the primary classrooms. Robinson and Robinson (1978a,b) found that it was possible to improve children's understanding of message failure by giving such explicit explanation.

Before this is used, as Tough (1977) does, to recommend devoting large amounts of class time in the primary classroom to explaining communication failure, it is worth pointing to one of Robinson's (1981a) other points. If success in communication were not the rule, why would the child seek to explain failure? The fact is that children learn a vast amount about the audiences for communication before they attend primary school with little explicit explanation.

The frequency of such explanations by adults is also rather insignificant. Like most other communication skills, momentary awareness that there is a problem and of a possible solution may possibly be a prerequisite for learning. Hearing or giving explicit verbal explanations are certainly not. The general message for teachers from these studies is, rather, to allow children to face as many problems of an appropriate level involving communication with audiences as possible. The experience of the difficulties encountered occasionally accompanied by verbal explanation of their nature, is probably the best way to help them succeed. It would also be wrong to give the impression that problems of ambiguity or audience assessment are the most difficult faced by the child. Lempers and Elrod (1983) discovered that children found messages involving unfamiliar vocabulary the most difficult to appraise of all the various sources of communication difficulty they investigated.

Turning more directly to writing problems, it has been common to think that one of the main problems children face in learning to write is to address an audience that is not in the here and now and may share much less common knowledge with the writer than people ordinarily do in conversation. Collins and Williamson (1981) give an example of this kind of initial writing difficulty: 'One night, me and my friends went to the store.' It isn't clear which night, which friends or which store. We find that more sophisticated versions of such difficulties in adapting to audience knowledge dog young writers until they become old writers!

Mosenthal and his associates have tried to map the development of adaptation to the potential reader.[8] They began by dividing young children's adaptation to audience in their spoken language into three varieties. The child's predominant style of coping with the audience problem in speaking was then related to their style of coping with this problem in writing.

In the imitative spoken style the child tends to parrot back teacher statements; such children tend to base the structure of their written texts on externally-given structures, and to narrative-based story-like organisation. In the noncontingent response register, the child tends to reply to the teacher with an unrelated remark or topic. Such children are claimed to structure stories according to preconceived ideas and to find adaptation to the particular demands of a new situation difficult. Finally, in the contingent response register children reply to the teacher by attempting to add to or clarify the teacher's remarks. When such children write they combine pre-existing schemas with the particular situation to produce a composite solution. How the practising teacher might respond to such different writing styles is at present unclear. Mosenthal *et al.* (1981) suggest they may be less evident in classroom situations than they are in experimental ones because adult expectations tend to be clearer in the former. Warnings against applying a standard prepared answer in exam situations are part of the secondary teacher's traditional craft. Presumably the child who writes in the noncontingent mode might benefit from more emphasis on this kind of difficulty, even at the primary level.

Many teachers using process writing approaches encourage students to be aware of audience problems by talking about the principles involved. Thus in response to the student who began 'One night me and my friends went to the store' we might hope that when the piece is discussed in conference the other students will pick up the problem. If they don't the teacher shouldn't be afraid to say 'Which friends did you go with?', and when the child replies the teacher might then ask 'Could I tell which friends you went with from what you wrote?' However, we don't want to press this sort of thing too far. The child is writing in a small, closed community (the classroom) and the intended audience might be a small group of friends who actually knew which friends went and which store they went to. Under these circumstances the piece is quite acceptable as a story told to friends. It may be worth pointing out that it is only the teacher who doesn't know this information. There will, however, undoubtedly arise situations where children forget to give information needed by the intended audience even if this is children. The important thing in teaching writing is not to discourage the child by excessive criticism and a sea of red ink, at the same time feeling free to give helpful hints when these will help in the solution of the problems immediately confronting the writer.

CONCLUSIONS

In the initial phases, learning to write, whether taught by process or traditional approaches, depends largely on acquiring skill in manipulating the pen and in spelling. As the writer becomes more proficient in these skills, problems of organising information for the reader come to the fore. Children can learn much from other students about when they are giving too much information and when they are giving too little. However, it is often difficult for other students to give a clear explanation of the principles that need to be applied to avoid such failures and clear explanations of these principles by teachers will be of help. It is hard to find a list of such principles written down that will be helpful to the primary teacher, but with repeated contact with examples of problems most teachers become aware of the most relevant ones. Some useful hints on this can be found in Graves (1983). In the top two years of the primary school, it is also desirable for students to think about using a plan for their writing, at least at second draft stage.

FURTHER READING

Beard (1984) provides an excellent general survey. Graves (1983) tells you how to implement the Graves approach and if read critically presents many stimulating ideas. Wilkinson *et al.* (1981) is well worth reading for the detailed, and often amusing, excerpts from children's work.

NOTES

1. See Nold (1981), Shaughnessy (1977), Flower and Hayes (1981a,b), Schumacher *et al.* (1984).
2. Auzai and Uchida (1981).
3. Maratsos (1973), Shatz and Gelman (1973).
4. Lawton (1968), Toomey (1974), Edwards (1976), Robinson (1978).
5. Toomey (1974), Wells (1981).
6. Robinson and Robinson (1977), Robinson and Robinson (1976a).
7. By Clough (1971) and Cambourne (1971).
8. For a survey see Mosenthal (1982).

Chapter 4

ART

CHILDREN'S REPRESENTATIONAL PAINTING AND DRAWING

Painting and drawing is called 'representational' when it tries to represent on paper people and things that exist in the world. The Piagetian approach to this topic is often summed up in the saying 'The child draws what it knows, not what it sees'. This dictum has had a considerable influence on the practice of teachers at both preschool and infant class levels. From the mid 1950s on, teachers were often advised not to show children how to draw and paint beyond demonstrating the way to hold the pencil and how to load and wash the brush. The rationale for this was that the limitations of the child's painting and drawing are the limitations of its thinking. When a child draws a person as two round shapes touching one another—one for the head and one for the body—this is because this is the way the child thinks about the human body. Of course the child can see more than this—children probably see the human body as well as an adult. But between seeing and the act of painting or drawing comes thinking or understanding. The child must first convert what is seen into thoughts or concepts and then draw these. According to Piaget and Inhelder one of the first things the child knows about space, for instance, is whether two objects touch or are separated. Hence the child's interest in representing the idea that the head touches the body.

From this approach it follows that because the child's thinking will advance only slowly as experience accumulates, it is pointless to show children how to paint or draw people or houses or trees. If we do this it will be an unnatural achievement, a kind of trick learned to please adults and without meaning for the child.

One of the chief messages of more recent work has been that Piaget and Inhelder probably underestimated the technical problems posed by painting and drawing. These technical difficulties are of two main varieties: the problem of moving the pencil or brush along a particular kind of path, such as a circle or a straight line; and the problem of showing three dimensional space using the two dimensions of the paper. In both these areas the child may need rather more help than Piaget and Inhelder implied. This does not of course mean that one should go back to the opposite extreme and show the child exactly how to do everything. Painting and drawing can develop as a balance between assistance and discovery without becoming a copying exercise.

This raises an interesting question: why shouldn't art be a copying exercise? In Australian Aboriginal culture, for instance, certain ways of picturing people and animals and a certain style in the use of line are more or less obligatory. Various standardised representations of the holy family and the saints were used in the ikon paintings of the Eastern Orthodox churches. Of course, artists in these traditions didn't copy their models down to the last detail—their art was to introduce individuality within the discipline of the tradition. But discipline and tradition had the upper hand and, particularly within Aboriginal culture, ego tripping was and is frowned upon. Modern Western painting, with its emphasis upon the self-expression of the individual artist and liberation from constraints, is at the opposite extreme. Yet even here we find admiration for the disciplined traditions of African art in artists like Picasso and Epstein.

As in several other areas Piaget has become identified with a kind of education that emphasises the self-development and self-discovery of the individual rather than the handing down of a tradition. One does not have to venture too far into sociology to see in some of the reactions against him a disillusion with the results of over-permissive upbringing and education and a desire for some stabilising sense of tradition and community.

Piaget and Inhelder's Contribution

In *The Child's Conception of Space* (1948) Piaget and Inhelder describe three stages in the development of drawings.

Stage 1: Synthetic Incapacity
They give as a typical example of the child's drawing at ages 3 and 4 years:

> a boy aged 3.6 who draws a man in the shape of a large head to which are appended four strokes, two representing the arms and two the legs, as well as a small trunk separate from the limbs. The head contains two eyes, a nose and a mouth, but the latter is placed above the former. (p. 46)

Piaget and Inhelder argue that to draw something when it is not present, the child must be able to construct a mental image of the object. They imply that the same thing happens even when the object is present, presumably because the child has to look at the paper while drawing. This image, they claim, depends very much on the child's level of conceptual development. The reason that the mouth is found above the nose is that the child has not yet conceptualised the vertical axis. In the absence of this, the child doesn't know exactly where to place the features.

There are five general principles that govern drawings at this stage.

1. *Proximity.* Generally the various parts of an object like the human body are drawn near to one another. In a drawing of a person, the head, body and limbs are all grouped near one another, though the limbs may be attached to the head and the body slightly separated from them.

2. *Separation.* The various parts of the body are not drawn on top of one another and this shows a realisation that they are separated in space.

3. *Order.* Shapes can be ordered two at a time on the paper, though even here there are often mistakes, as when a dog's tail, which should be on the right, is attached to its head, on the left. The difficulty of ordering shapes when more than two are involved can be seen from the example of the mouth that came above the nose. We may imagine the child realised that the nose was below the eyes and that the mouth was below the eyes. She forgot to check that the mouth was below the nose.

4. *Enclosure.* Though the features often appear jumbled up inside the circle that makes the head, the child has realised that they go inside the head and not outside. Likewise buttons go inside the body, though in both cases errors are still made.

5. *Continuity and discontinuity.* Different parts of the same body generally touch one another, though sometimes, as with the body separated from the head, this is forgotten. Similarly a rider may remain suspended above his horse or a hat above a head. The rider, the horse, the hat and the head are continuous objects, while the gaps symbolise the discontinuity between them. The difference between drawing a continuous line for an arm and drawing a number of little circles for buttons also seems to illustrate this.

Stage 2: Intellectual Realism

From about 5-7 or 8 years we find drawings that are much more easily recognised as representing 'a man', 'a house' or 'a car'. The chief difficulty now is in co-ordinating the various objects in the picture. Often objects are drawn from a number of contradictory perspectives. Thus a horse may be shown side-on, but its carriage head-on. Houses and people are shown side-on or front-on in a street plan that seems to have been drawn from the air. Relative sizes and distances are also a problem: cars and people are bigger than houses; the houses are all bunched up at one end of the street and widely spaced at the other without any intention to convey perspective—the child has just failed to cope with the idea of an even separation.

These characteristics are explained as the result of two achievements. The child can now cope effectively with the problems of proximity, separation, order and enclosure. This accounts for the more recognisable people, animals and houses, with noses above mouths, tails on the rear ends of dogs, chimneys attached to roofs. The child is now learning to tackle sizes, distances and perspectives, but still makes many mistakes.

Stage 3: Visual Realism
At about 8 or 9 years the child learns to successfully manage relative sizes and shapes and to co-ordinate perspectives. Thus all the adults in the drawing are of the same size, children being somewhat smaller and houses somewhat larger. When a car is drawn from the side its driver must also appear from the side.

The child's understanding of perspective was studied in particular detail. Children were asked what shape an object such as a needle or a disc will appear to be when viewed from different angles by a doll. It is not until about age 9 years that children say that the needle seen end-on and the disc seen side-on will appear as a dot and a line respectively. At 7 and 8 years they tend to say that as the doll moves round the needle looks like a shorter and shorter line. But the child cannot visualise that when the doll sees only the end of the needle it will appear as a point. Instead the child says it appears as a short line. Similarly at this stage the disc seen from the side appears as a thin elipse.

However, when children still at this intermediate stage were shown a stick end-on they could correctly draw it as a dot or small circle (pp. 185-6). Piaget and Inhelder do not make much of this point, but it seems to show that the problem of drawing from life is somewhat easier than the purely conceptual problem of imagining what a doll will see. The child may improve a little on what it knows from what it sees.

Children were also asked to draw a road and a railway line receding into the distance. Here it is claimed the children were generally 9 years of age before they could draw the sides of the road converging and the railway sleepers getting progressively shorter.

A Cross-Cultural Extension

Hess-Behrens (1974) used Piaget and Inhelder's analysis of children's art to look at children from a variety of cultural groups in Brazil, Denmark, Germany, Greenland, Hong Kong, India, Italy and the USA. All groups were found to progress through the stages outlined by Piaget and Inhelder, which they themselves developed from the earlier work of Luquet (1913, 1927), except that a group of non-literate, rural Amazon Indians showed very little evidence of a transition from intellectual realism to visual realism. Hess-Behrens also notes that 'Nearly all elements in the Amazon

Indian drawings appear as stylised forms or as signs. Without familiarity with this idiom, particular species (of animals) often could not be distinguished, nor could sign meanings be understood.'

While upper and middle-class groups consistently passed through these stages more rapidly in Denmark, India, Italy and the US, such differences did not occur in Greenland, Germany and Japan. This is explained in terms of the greater sense of social cohesion and lack of an alienated working or 'lower' class in the latter countries. Differences in art provision in different kinds of schools were also found to have an effect. In Hong Kong this was particularly visible. Class differences in progress there persist until junior high school, corresponding to the lack of art provision in schools with a largely working-class intake. Such provision is made in the junior high school, and here differences disappear.

Reconsidering Piaget and Inhelder

Two lines of argument have figured prominently in recent discussions of children's drawing. One is summarised by Booth (1975), who reviewed a number of diary studies of early drawing. She found that children's first drawings progressing beyond scribble were generally attempts to copy adult demonstrations of how to draw things. This is something that tends to be missed by preschool teachers who are often unaware of what kind of demonstrations are provided at home. Booth has furthermore shown in a number of studies of painting in infant classes that if the teacher avoids asking 'Can you tell me what it is?', or other encouragement to produce representations, children tend to gravitate towards pattern painting rather than painting representing people and things. These observations lead Booth to conclude that representational drawing is at least partly learned from adults and other children in the early stages.

Another line of evidence, emphasised by Freeman (1977, 1980), comes from studies of figure completion. Freeman showed children such things as a face with a body but not arms and legs. Without prompting some children attached the arms and legs to the body. But some of these children would attach the arms to the head when drawing a whole figure for themselves. It seems that attaching the arms to the head is not ignorance about where the arms go. The child is not 'drawing what it knows'. Rather some technical problem with the actual process of drawing causes these children to attach the arms to the head when they know quite well they should be attached to the body. Freeman also found that children who could only scribble on their own could add arms, legs and facial features to two circles already provided as head and body. The child may know more than it draws.

These observations should make us pause and think more closely about what might be happening when children draw things. Two alternatives to the Piaget and Inhelder argument present themselves. One is that the child doesn't really think about the spatial construction of the object being drawn at all. Rather the child thinks 'I want to draw a person' and then proceeds to reel off a series of actions that make marks on the paper that end up looking like a person. Thus the child might begin with the circle for the head, add the body, then the limbs and then the facial features. While this has been a widely-held view of early representational drawings, Van Sommers (1983, 1984) has shown that if children are asked to draw the same object repeatedly they draw it in roughly the same way, but they seldom use the same sequence of actions to do it. He concludes they must be remembering a visual image of the stereotype they produce and then producing this by a relatively flexible process. However, flexibility is not entirely incompatible with an emphasis on the importance of sequencing major items in the drawing. Thus Golomb (1983) found that in drawing the human figure there is a strong sequence in the production of the main body parts, with head coming first, then body, then arms, then legs. This is often accompanied by a return or returns upwards to fill in details such as facial features, hair, ears and clothing. It is largely the process of filling in minor detail that results in flexibility, while the production of major body parts is done in a fairly standard order.

Another possibility is that the child does think about the real object but is confused by the problem of getting a three-dimensional object onto two-dimensional paper. Most children's early drawings show the human figure from the front, which seems to be an easy view to draw. It may be that they need to be shown that this is an easy way to do it.

Whether we choose these approaches or some even more elaborate model, the problem of coping with the space on the paper is likely to be an important one. The child is having to cope with 'what goes where' on the paper. This was something also emphasised by Piaget and Inhelder. The body is below the head, eyes are above the nose, arms are horizontal and attached to the body, legs are vertical and attached to the body. We know from Freeman's observations of children completing figures that they do know about things like this, however much they may at times seem to reel off their figures without any thought at all.

Another problem that is likely to be important whichever view we take is that of getting the actions into some order and then remembering to do all of them. The object that is to be drawn exists in space as a head above a body, a nose above a mouth, arms attached to body, etc. The process of drawing has to start somewhere. The child might, for instance, begin from the mouth and then put in a leg. But this would create a problem: whereabouts on the paper should the leg go? To get the drawing right the child would have to estimate how big the body will be and then draw it in later. In practice the temptation will arise for the leg to be attached to the mouth. Rolf Harris can fill in the missing parts of a surprisingly disjointed body. Children will tend to attach the next element to something already on the paper. Perhaps that is why children are tempted to attach the arms to the head: they thought of adding on the arms when only the head was on the paper. Observation of how children draw suggests that once a mistake of this kind has been made it can become for a while part of a stereotyped way of drawing a person. But a time will inevitably come when this is felt to be inadequate and efforts at re-organisation set in. In the problem of sequencing we can see another reason why adult or child demonstrations may be important: the child picks up clues as to where to start and how to carry on from there. Booth (1975) found that it was demonstrations and not copying from pictures that had already been drawn that was important.

These arguments are still too simple. We can quite often find children attaching the arms to the head of their drawings even after they have drawn the body. Furthermore these children, like others who attach hands to bodies, can sometimes get the attachment right when provided with a ready-drawn head and body. However, Freeman (1975) has found that children who attach the arms wrongly in their own drawings, or can only scribble, usually attach the arms to the body of a ready-made head and body only if the body is considerably bigger than the head. If the head is considerably bigger than the body then the arms are attached to the head. Now children who attach arms to the head in their own drawings ('tadpole' drawers) usually draw the head much bigger than the body. One reason for this is probably that the head is usually the first thing to be drawn and the child is not constrained either by space or by having to join it up to anything else. So the arms may get attached to the head partly because it is bigger than the body. Freeman suggests that children may go for the larger shape to attach the arms to because it provides a bigger target to hit. The child is in effect attending to the problem of making sure that the arms are properly joined on to something and in the enthusiasm to get this right forgets about joining them on to the right thing.

Other important technical influences on children's drawing are their preferences for the horizontal and vertical directions and for judgements based on parallels or right angles.

Emphasis on the problems that the child encounters on the paper should not, however, blind us to the possibility of getting the child to think about the thing being drawn. Teachers often question children to encourage realisations about the thing drawn and its relation to the drawing. In the case of arms attached to heads the question might be as to where the child's own arms join on to its body. Such questions sometimes lead to changes in the next drawing, but often not, especially in the earlier stages. Yet there does come a point at which children begin to be dissatisfied with the realism of their drawings. A good example of this is shown in Figure 1. Here Marie has begun from the usual stereotype of how to draw a house, with a pointed roof, two side walls and a floor. But she is dissatisfied with this because it isn't like her own block of flats. So she has assembled a number of other features inside it: many storeys, with steps between them, many people and many television sets. Notice that the stairs have been shown as ladders, presumably because she knew how to draw ladders. Yet the way the elements have been arranged inside the block of flats quite clearly shows Marie's knowledge about them. She has moved on from learning how to draw individual things to learning how to arrange them to show scenes and situations. She was not shown how to arrange the elements in the flats: she made that up for herself. While this drawing is unusually inventive, children at Piaget and Inhelder's stage of intellectual realism typically draw scenes showing mummy going for a walk with the dog and the pram or someone catching a particularly big fish. These are often remembered events that have never been drawn or painted before. In this sense the child really is 'drawing what it knows'.

Fig. 1. *My house, by Marie aged 6 years*

However, it would be misleading to think that having attained intellectual realism the child's difficulties now stem entirely from problems of knowing about the real world. Piaget and Inhelder say 'One finds in one and the same drawing evidence of a jumble of irreconcilable points of view.' (p. 50) They imply that it is the inability of the child to relate points of view in the real world, as when the child fails to imagine correctly what another person can see, that leads to these difficulties. Yet we have already encountered another very powerful reason for them: the stereotyped way that the child learns to draw individual objects. When we find a street plan drawn from the air and people walking in the streets drawn from the front and sides this may be simple inability to draw any other views of the people. The same argument applies in reverse to the streets. They are not drawn from the side because that would require representation of depth and we know most children don't begin to grasp that until about 8 or 9 years of age. The child's drawing at this point is certainly limited by what is not known—perspective. But what is drawn stems more from a technical problem: many objects and plans are most easily drawn from a certain angle. People are most easily drawn from the front, streets from above, cars from the side. When all these easily drawn perspectives are put together we do get a jumble of perspectives, but not quite for the reason Piaget and Inhelder give.

The achievement of perspective has been significantly clarified by Willats (1977), who distinguishes a number of ways in which children may attempt to represent three dimensional space on a two dimensional page. These are as follows. In vertical oblique projection, lines coming towards the observer are shown as parallel and vertical. Thus the table shown in Figure 2 would be drawn as indicated.

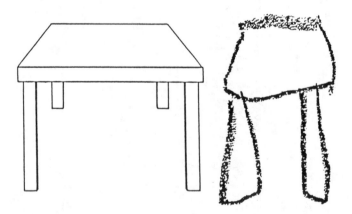

Fig. 2. *Vertical Oblique Projection of a Table*

In oblique projection lines coming towards the observer are still shown as parallel, but are at an oblique angle. Thus the top of a table becomes a parallelogram.

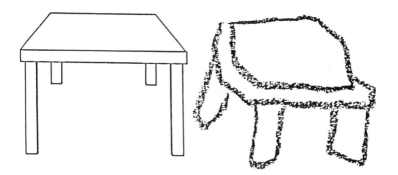

Fig. 3. *Oblique Projection of a Table*

In orthogonal projection lines coming towards the observer appear as points. This is a common starting point for young children.

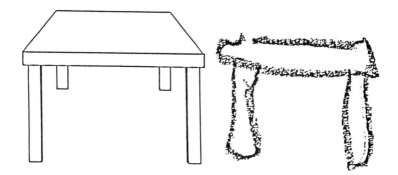

Fig. 4. *Orthogonal Projection of a Table*

In occlusion a nearer object is shown partly obscuring a further object. Young children tend to avoid depicting this. Finally we have the means of representing depth most approved by realistic Western drawing: perspective. Here lines going away from the observer are shown converging to a point (Figure 5). This may still involve some distortion of the scene witnessed by the eye.

In his study of children's drawings from 5-17 years Willats found that the mean age of children using no means to represent depth was 7.4 years; the mean age of those using orthographic projection was 9.7 years; the mean age of those using vertical oblique projection was 11.9 years; for oblique projection the mean was 13.6 years; for perspective about 14 years. Only half the adolescents surveyed between 15½ and 17½ years could use perspective. The number of occlusions used in the drawings rose as children grew older. Children below the age of 9 made little use of occlusion, while by 12 years nearly all seen overlaps were drawn.

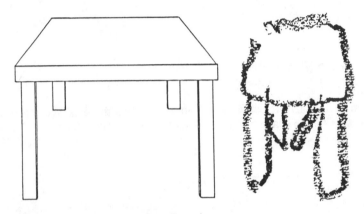

Fig. 5. *Distorted Perspective Drawing*

Willats points out that we cannot assume that the child learns perspective drawing purely by a process of discovery. Oblique projection was adopted as the basis for perspective drawing by adults in traditional Chinese and Japanese painting. Progress towards perspective drawing must partly depend upon seeing adult pictures using this system, introduced into Western drawing in the Italian Renaissance. Comparing one's own efforts with adult pictures and explicit teaching of the rules of perspective are two processes that may be involved here. At the same time he claims there must be an element of discovery present as Western children seldom see adult pictures based on orthogonal or either of the oblique projection systems. This is actually incorrect as the 'pictograms' that adults use to demonstrate drawing to young children involve orthogonal projection, though the point is well taken regarding oblique projections.

Cox (1978) found that children as young as 5 years will attempt to represent depth relationships between objects in drawings, when these are drawn to their attention, though such efforts are initially rudimentary, as when the farther object is shown above the nearer one. Light and Simmons (1983) encouraged children to represent depth by occlusion (the nearer object blocking out the farther) with a communication game in which another child had to identify the chair the drawer was sitting on when making the drawing. This helped 7 and 8 year olds, but not 5 and 6 year olds.

Alland (1983) further reinforced the conclusion that children learn much about drawing from cultural influences by comparing children's drawing in different cultures. Thus the rules for making a picture in Bali were: 'Begin anywhere; using many colors cover the page with marks, or simple units (circles, for example); do not allow these to touch. As space becomes filled, search for open space and fill with marks of decreasing size.' (p. 215) Whereas in Ponape, another island in South-East Asia, the rules are: 'Make a mark or simple unit on the page. Build the picture outward from this starting point, but, as the picture builds outward, close back on it . . . There is no strong page-filling imperative in Ponape.' (p. 215)

NON-REPRESENTATIONAL PAINTING AND DRAWING

Non-representational painting or drawing is art that explores the possibilities of pattern and design on the paper without attempting to depict or represent things in the world like people, animals or houses. This is in effect an easier spatial problem for children as it gets rid of the need to relate a three-dimensional world to two-dimensional paper. The child can explore the possibilities of the two-dimensional paper unhampered.

Piaget and Inhelder did not comment on this kind of drawing and painting, though its existence was certainly recognised by Luquet and other early students of child art. It seems, however, not to have been as common among children's paintings before World War II as it has since become. One of the reasons for this increase has been the advice of Rhoda Kellogg and others not to ask children 'What is it?' or to encourage representational painting in other ways.

Kellogg (1970) believes that early drawing is fundamentally non-representational. When children scribble and experiment with making different shapes on the paper they are, to her, primarily interested in marks on the paper. Their tendency to say 'It's a bird' or 'It's mummy' comes from adult encouragement. In support of this we may also cite Booth's (1975, 1981) studies showing that classroom painting tends towards pattern making when there is no adult pressure for representation. This, however, does not show that when children are encouraged to relate their drawings to objects in the world they fail to make any real connection between the marks on the paper and a bird or mummy.

It is true that at first the act of representation seems to be a complete fiction. The child points to a scribble one day and says 'bird'; the next day a similar or even the same scribble may be called 'mummy'. The scribble shows no likeness to the thing it represents. Soon, however, some distinction appears: rounded shapes may be people and short, straight lines birds. At this point it is hard not to believe that the child is really relating the shape to the thing represented. There remains, however, the possibility that the child makes the shape first and then attaches the name as an afterthought, either through hearing it named by an adult or through noticing some similarity with the object.

Kellogg's claim that the investigation of pattern and shape is primary is at best unproven. It is hard to know what children's intentions really are when they draw and paint or where they get their ideas from. It does, however, draw support from two observations about children's drawing. They often draw without naming the shape drawn and may resist naming it if asked; and the problem of making shapes on the paper is itself a difficult one—we would expect children to be drawn to this problem and to neglect the much more difficult one of relating this to a three dimensional world.

Kellogg's argument works quite well for the young child. But by the time children get to the age of 5 or 6 years we often see a marked split between work that can be clearly labelled as 'pattern' and work that can be clearly labelled as 'picture'. Sometimes a pattern is introduced into a picture of a scene, as when the sun is drawn as a number of coloured circles inside one another, but generally the two are quite separate. Booth (1981) found that among 156·5 year old primary school children, given no teacher encouragement to produce representations, 141 produced paintings that could be clearly categorised as representational as well as paintings that could be clearly categorised as pattern. Eight children produced paintings that could be categorised as a mixture of pattern and representation, as well as paintings that were clearly patterns. Only three children produced entirely patterns. For this reason we should accept Booth's argument that at least by school age the majority of children have developed a fairly clear separation between patterns and representations, at least in the realm of painting.

Kellogg was among the first to analyse pattern making in detail.[1] Booth's (1981) study has, however, considerably refined her analyses by following the progress of individual children over time. Furthermore, while Kellogg points out that children make patterns by putting lines and shapes together, Booth (1975, 1981) added to this by investigating how the lines and shapes are put together using pattern-making operations. Like Freeman (1980), Booth emphasises the need to watch the sequence of steps the child goes through in executing a painting. She uses this to discover the actual operations used in making the pattern. Using these methods Booth (1981) has distinguished the following sequence of pattern-making stages. These are stages in the sense that children very rarely experiment with a higher stage without having experimented with the lower stages leading up to it. We do, however, find many instances of children falling back to a lower stage for a while before resuming work at the higher stage.

The Scribble Stage

At this stage children scribble on the paper. With paint, the result of adding different colours on top of one another while still wet, will often be a brown pool in the middle of the paper.

The Topology Stage

This corresponds to Piaget and Inhelder's stage of synthetic incapacity at which proximity, separation, order, enclosure, continuity and discontinuity are explored. In painting this typically takes the form of an attempt to divide up the paper into a number of irregular areas of different colour, thus showing interest in proximity and separation. At the same time the method of applying colour changes from the continuous oscillating stroke to single strokes. Developing from these single strokes comes the use of dots and lines. Dots are often scattered at random inside each irregular coloured area; sometimes a blank page may be covered with an irregular scatter of dots. Both these types of painting show an interest in the enclosure of the dots within an area and possibly in the contrast between the continuously coloured areas and the discontinuity of the dots. When the stage is well established the dots may be lined up in orderly rows, an action that foreshadows the pattern-making activities of the next stage.

The Pattern-Making Stage

Patterns in two dimensions made by young children are of two main kinds: divisions of the plane, and those formed by pattern-making operations. A typical division of the plane is to paint in the diagonals of a rectangular sheet of paper. This may be followed by further elaborations (Figure 6). The basic pattern-making operations are those of translation, reflection and rotation (Figure 7). In translation an element such as a dot or line is repeated at regular intervals, usually across or down the paper. In reflection an element appears on one side of the paper and its mirror image on the other side. In rotation an element appears rotated several times through roughly the same angle. Rotation patterns are less common than the other types.

The pattern-making operations show the same interest in constructing equal lengths and angles as Piaget and Inhelder noted in representational painting at their stage of intellectual realism, lasting from approximately 5-8 years. This is also the age at which the pattern-making operations are found.

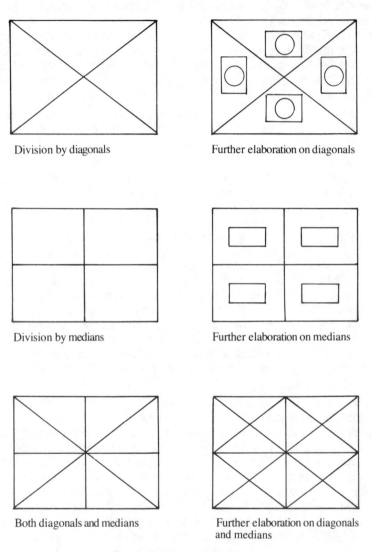

Division by diagonals

Further elaboration on diagonals

Division by medians

Further elaboration on medians

Both diagonals and medians

Further elaboration on diagonals
and medians

Fig. 6. *Divisions of the Plane*

The first patterns to appear are usually those based on the translation of lines or dots. Thus we get equally spaced horizontal or vertical lines and equally spaced rows of dots or other shapes. Another pattern that often appears early is a wavy line whose right-hand end is the mirror image of its left-hand end. Patterns using divisions of the plane, rotation or combinations of different types of operation usually appear later, as do those in which a row of dots is itself repeated at regular intervals across or down the paper.

DOES ART HELP CHILDREN TO THINK?

Because Piaget and Inhelder assumed that children thought about real space when they painted or drew it was natural for people to think that art helped children to think about real space. More recent discussions have undermined this assumption. The difficulty faced by children is less that of understanding the world than of understanding the paper. But perhaps in understanding the two-dimensional paper the child is in effect experimenting with a simplified space and this might enable it to make discoveries about this simplified space that can later be extended to three-dimensional space. Perhaps children understand things like equal lengths, equal angles and parallel lines more easily through experimenting with them in art. There is a moderate correlation between tests of spatial concepts and painting achievement (Booth, 1981). But it may be that achievement on the spatial concepts tests and painting achievement are both reflections of a common underlying spatial ability. At present the case for saying that painting and drawing helps children think remains unproven.

CONCLUSIONS

The advice to teachers that was derived from Piagetian theory for teaching representational painting and drawing was based on the motto 'The child draws what it knows'. The motto that arises from more recent research in this area is 'The child draws what it knows how to draw'. At most periods in their development children draw using both skills centered on the paper and skills centered on the relation between the paper and the world. In both areas there is now evidence that children normally learn a good deal by demonstrations and advice from parents and other children and it probably hinders the child's development if teachers refuse requests for help with the technical aspects of drawing. Both demonstrations of how to draw things and discussions of how to draw them are helpful, though children also need a good deal of time to experiment with new techniques.

Translation

Vertical translation of lines

Horizontal translation of circle

Reflection

Reflection in a vertical axis

Reflection in a horizontal axis

Rotation

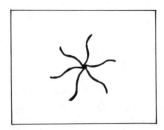

Rotation about a point

Fig. 7. *The Pattern-Making Operations*

Children seem able to progress through the stages of non-representational painting and drawing more easily without outside assistance and in most schoolrooms they will pick up enough from other children without explicit help from the teacher, though discussion of matters raised by the child should not be discouraged.

FURTHER READING

The best books on representational drawing are Freeman (1980) and Van Sommers (1984). Willats (1977), Davis (1985) and Light and Foot (1986) are well worth looking at on perspective; Alland (1983) is an interesting cross-cultural study and Ives (1984) is interesting on the expression of emotion. Booth's work on non-representational painting is outlined in Booth (1982) and Booth (1984); those with a more serious interest would need to order her (1975) or (1981) theses.

NOTE

1. Kellogg and O'Dell (1967), Kellogg (1970).

Chapter 5

SCIENCE

INTRODUCTION

This chapter will cover the areas of classification, causality and children's physics. Once again Piaget and his collaborators were among the first to investigate these areas. The main results of more recent work have been to alter some Piagetian conclusions about the descriptions he offered of children's thinking and to throw considerable doubt on his views about learning. Both these issues have been dealt with in a general fashion in the Introduction and the conclusions outlined there can be read off fairly directly to deal with science teaching. More specifically, recent work has indicated that Piaget's ideas about classification in the preschool child tended to underplay the very young child's abilities. However, when we reach the school-age child, Piagetian descriptive conclusions are still valid for most practical purposes. Piaget also tended to underestimate the causal reasoning abilities of children up to 7 or 8 years of age.

Recent investigations of children's physics have reported studies in a number of areas such as gravity and electricity that were not dealt with by Piaget in any significant detail. As far as teaching concepts is concerned Karplus's learning cycle provides a useful guideline, with its three phases of exploration (unaided experimentation with problems), explicit teaching of concepts or principles and finally application of the principles to practical examples.

CLASSIFICATION

At around the age of 7 or 8 many children become interested in forming collections of things, such as stamps, coins, butterflies, birds' eggs or other collectables. Such collections will usually involve at least a one-way classification, as when stamps or coins are categorised according to their country of origin. Sometimes sub-hierarchies may appear within these major groups, as when the amount of money denoted by a stamp or coin is used to arrange the items by denomination within countries. Such classifications using sub-hierarchies are also involved in science classes when the distinctions between phyla, genera and species of animals are taught. More informally, a study of insects in a pond may yield 'pond insects' and this sub-category of insects can then be broken down into the various species of insect found.

Classifications of this kind are clearly very important in science and they provide a level of scientific thinking that can be assimilated in the upper primary classes. As in other areas the work of Piaget and his collaborators was responsible for stimulating interest in children's understanding of classification. Inhelder and Piaget (1964) published a series of experiments investigating classificatory thinking in children. The key studies dealt with 'spontaneous classification', in which children are given a collection of objects and asked to 'Put together things that are alike'. For instance, in one study children were given materials consisting of squares, triangles, rings and half-rings (dimension of shape); wood or plastic (dimension of material); and blue, red, yellow or green (dimension of colour). In general it was not until around 4½ that children could arrange such shapes along one dimension (e.g. sorting objects into piles by colour—a pile of blue objects, a pile of red objects, etc.). It was not until around 7 years that objects could be cross-classified along two dimensions simultaneously. An example of this would be by colour and shape, with first blue squares, then blue triangles, then blue rings, passing on to red squares, red triangles, red rings and so forth. In between these two points we find the emergence of 'shifting'. Children of 4½-5 years, approximately, will be able to sort along the dimension of, say, colour, but when asked 'Can you do it another way?', they are stumped. After about 5 years, following such a request, children are able to shift to another dimension but cannot sort using both simultaneously. It seems that shifting is a step on the road from one-dimensional to two-dimensional classification.[1] Cross-classification is slightly different from the use of sub-hierarchies so often found in science, but Inhelder and Piaget (1964) found that when materials for spontaneous classification were hierarchically structured, ability to undertake sorting also emerged around 7 years.

Inhelder and Piaget (1964) found that the nature of the materials given for the sorting had an influence on the difficulty of classifications. Coloured geometrical shapes and pictures of flowers were equally easy, but pictures of animals were more difficult. This, they speculate, may have been due to the unfamiliarity of the animals for city children (*ibid.*, Chapter 4).

The validity of this sequence in broad outline has not been effectively contested, particularly as regards the later stages. Some pertinent criticism has been made of their account of the earliest period preceding one-dimensional classification. This is a period that Inhelder and Piaget (1964) termed one of 'graphic collections'. Here children were claimed to either make patterns from the objects to be classified or to organise collections based on an unsystematic and 'illogical' shifting of criteria.[2] This account has been thrown into doubt by a number of studies which concluded that very young children tend to classify things on the basis of 'natural categories'.[3] Rather than attempting to separate categories on a hard-and-fast criterion (these are all large, these are all small) natural categories try to separate categories that are 'information rich'. For instance, if we want to separate birds from mammals by a strict, biological definition we say that birds have feathers and lay eggs, while mammals do not have feathers, do not lay eggs and suckle their young. However, young children tend to separate them by thinking that birds have feathers, lay eggs, fly, have beaks and two legs, while mammals are furry, do not lay eggs, do not fly, have noses and four legs. This second way of making the distinction is inaccurate but it is also more useful for practical purposes and usually gets the right answer. It is often hard to find out at a glance if something lays eggs, while most birds fly and most mammals don't. So if you assemble a whole bundle of things that something must have to be a bird or a mammal and you find it has most of them, you will usually be right—though not always.

So far I have been speaking as if early classifications based on natural categories and not involving dimensions are later superceded by classifications based upon the systematic use of dimensions and the strict application of rules. There is, however, growing agreement in the literature on classification learning that even after the ability to undertake orderly, one-dimensional and two-dimensional sortings appears, both children and adults continue to use a large number of ill-defined categories, particularly in the area of vocabulary. The reader may like to try as an exercise to define 'funeral', 'label' or 'boredom' using strict criteria. Even in the case of categories for which we can give a strict definition that most adults would know it seems that the definition is not the only thing used to define the category. Thus Smith *et al.* (1974) found that adults took less time to verify that 'robin' is a bird than that 'penguin' is a bird. This appears to be because robins are closer to the 'prototype' of a bird than penguins. This prototype involves the feature 'flies' even though not all birds fly. This kind of result has given new impetus to long-standing attempts to explain the interaction between strict definitions and the formation of prototypes in classification learning.[4] At present there has been little attempt to produce a theory of the developmental aspects of prototype formation in children, but this is an area in which we may expect to see developments in the future. It is, however, worth pointing out that 'natural categories' are based on finding that things like furriness, four-leggedness and having a certain kind of nose are often found together. This is just the kind of concept we would expect to be formed on the basis of continually associating these three kinds of judgement together. This naturally raises the question of how children ever go beyond such associative thinking. One theory is that it is because they begin to shift attention from immediate aspects of things like animals to the dimensions that connect such things, like size, shape, colour, texture and so forth. At the same time they try to be more exhaustive about their judgements. Instead of being satisfied with a definition of mammal that is right some of the time they demand one that is right all the time.

I now turn to studies more explicitly related to education. An analysis of hierarchical classification skills has been developed in relation to science teaching by Lowell (1977, 1979, 1980). Unlike Inhelder and Piaget (1964), Lowell considers two kinds of class inclusion that differ in level of abstraction. His Level V involves classes that are relatively narrow in scope and thus more concrete. The example given is that the biological category Hominoids subsumes both Hominids (man-like creatures) and Pongids (ape-like creatures). Level VI, on the other hand, 'refers to extremely broad generalized categories'. The example given is that the class of Mammals subsumes those of Anthropoids and Non-Anthropoid Mammals. As well as seeing if children could already cope with a given type of hierarchy Lowell also went on to teach these concepts. He found that Level V was indeed rather easier to achieve than Level VI. It was also notable that even among American high school students from 14.11-18.5 years it took an average of just over seven trials to reach a criterion for success at Level V and an average of just over ten to reach such a criterion at Level VI. The testing procedure used here for Level V was to show the child two objects, such as samples of the minerals galena (a lead ore) and quartz (a non-metallic mineral). The student was then shown a further box of six objects and asked to select samples of a metallic and of a non-metallic mineral from the new box and name them as belonging to these categories. For Level VI the child would be shown, for instance, galena (a mineral) and raffia (a living product). The classes 'mineral' and 'living product' are much broader than those of 'ore' and 'non-metallic mineral', thus making the mineral-living product distinction Level VI, while the difference between ore and non-metallic product is at Level V.

It is significant that in this study some students probably had to learn the contents of the classification as well as its form, that is the names and definitions of particular classes as well as how to deal with classes in general. The study is notable both for showing that more inclusive and abstract categories cause greater difficulty and that they can be taught.[5] Lowell found, in fact, that even students from 9.0-10.4 years could learn the Level VI task in just over twelve trials. The message for teachers would seem to be that while children of over about 9 years have trouble with some classifications they can quite rapidly be taught them.

Surprisingly, Lowell (1980) found that among American high school students it was not until about age 14 years that the average student could master a battery of tests of hierarchical classification ability. He suggests that this late grasp of such concepts compared with Inhelder and Piaget's (1964) subjects, who could master most of the tasks by around 9 or 10 years, may be a product of cultural and schooling differences between the United States and Geneva. While other studies on American children also indicate that they may experience difficulties with class inclusion and hierarchical classification up to 10 or 11 years, Lowell's study appears to show an unusually large discrepancy.[6] Reviews of this area point to the strong influence of materials and testing details on classification abilities and these may have contributed to Lowell's (1980) result.[7] In general, children in the UK have been found to resemble Genevan rather than US children in classification abilities.

Another study with an educational orientation was that of Lawton and Wanska (1979). These authors gave children from kindergarten to fifth grade initial tests for hierarchical classification and cross-classification. Only those who experienced difficulty with these skills went on to the teaching experiment. In the experiment children were either given instruction in the content of classification systems dealing with human evolution, taught the generalised classification skills described by Inhelder and Piaget (1964) or both. It was found that the combination of content and generalised skills resulted in more improvement on a subsequent test than either taught separately.

As in other areas, training studies have been generally successful in promoting classification learning.[8] Teaching by showing students an adult or child model performing the task has been particularly popular. Another method, used by Lawton and Wanska (1979), is to give the rules for sorting to children, have them sort and then correct sorting errors later with explanations. A slight elaboration of this method that would come naturally to teachers would be to use a diagram on the board while explaining the rules for assignment. Such a diagram might, for instance, show a branching tree going downwards, with higher-order classes represented by nodes at the top and component classes by nodes lower down.

CAUSALITY

We can conveniently divide children's causal explanations into two major categories: those that resemble scientists' causal explanations and those that are normally condemned by Western science as 'illogical' and invalid. Piaget (1929, 1930) identified a number of explanations of the first type: by natural law (e.g. paper burns, therefore this paper will burn); by contact (e.g. the various moving parts of a machine like a bicycle must touch one another to transmit force); by force (the forces acting on the parts of a bicycle are again an example). Since that time two other properties of correct causal reasoning have also been widely discussed: temporal precedence (a cause must come before or simultaneously with its effect); co-variation (for a single sufficient cause the cause must always be followed by the effect; for a number of jointly sufficient causes the whole bundle of causes must always be followed by the effect). Among the unscientific kinds of causation Piaget (1929, 1930) found in children, the most prominent were: animism (explanation that an inanimate object moves because it is alive and endowed with motives, goals or feelings); artificialism (natural formations like seas or mountains were created by human construction); finalism (things occur because of their beneficial effects, e.g. flowers bloom to look nice); magical similarity (a cause is the cause of its effect because it resembles the effect, e.g. dogs run about on the earth and make the clouds run about in the sky); transductive thinking (reasoning from one aspect of A to the same aspect of B and then trying to connect A and C by using a different aspect of B to compare with C); dynamism (agencies like fire or ice have the power to make and move the wind or the sea); and phenomenism (if two things regularly happen together one is the cause of the other, regardless of the physical connection between them, e.g. it rains because the sun goes in).

Two items on this second list of explanation types are not entirely frowned upon by Western science—finalism and phenomenism. Aristotle listed teleology (explanation in terms of the final outcome of processes) as one of his four kinds of correct causality, which is similar to finalism. Philosophers of science often condemn this kind of reasoning, but some find it useful (e.g. Whitehead, 1938, Chapter 8). Phenomenism is a much more widely accepted form of causality, particularly in physics, where Newton's acceptance that gravity is a force that acts at a distance led to the general acceptance that contact of bodies is not necessary for one to influence the other. Once we remove the requirement that bodies must touch, systematic co-variation becomes the major criterion for causality. Thus we say that the phases of the moon cause spring and neap tides on the earth although the moon does not touch the earth; the height of tides co-varies exactly with the movement of the moon around the earth. It must be recognised, however, that the co-occurrence often accepted by children as a criterion for causality is a lot looser than that required by a scientist.

Piaget (1929, 1930) argued that until 6 or 7 years of age most children's ideas about causality are of the non-scientific variety and can be described by the second list of terms just outlined. This contention generated much controversy in the 1930s and 1940s, notable critics being Isaacs (1930) and Huang et al. (1945). Laurendeau and Pinard (1962) and Piaget (1967) reviewed this literature and the former also conducted replication studies. Both concluded that those reporting results giving a more favourable impression of the young child's grasp of causality had not used Piaget's method of scoring results and that those supporting him had. From this both concluded that Piaget had been right. However, Piaget's scoring methods are open to serious objection.[9] Throughout his two books, if the child gives a non-scientific explanation at some point in the interview, say one based on animism or magical thinking, that child is scored as manifesting a 'pre-operational' and non-scientific mentality. However, the same child often manifests examples of the scientific attitude, such as explanations based on general laws or on contact. Taking this into account, there is little conflict in the literature over the nature of the younger child's thinking. At 3 or 4 years it is a mixture of scientific and unscientific notions in which the unscientific forms predominate and in which fundamentally different kinds of explanation will be offered for the same phenomenon at different times. By 7 or 8 years the incidence of the 'unscientific' explanations has declined considerably when the child is brought up in a Western society. Some vestiges of the unscientific types of explanation do, however, persist into adulthood, particularly in relation to unfamiliar phenomena.

Piaget's work is also rather misleading in dealing with the notion of a physical law in children. He argues here that while children often give explanations couched in terms of laws (e.g. wet things don't burn), such explanations are based on the model of social laws and are thus not true expressions of the concept of physical law. His argument here seems quite forced as what the children say is indistinguishable from the kind of explanations using laws given by adults.

Piaget's own observations serve to highlight the use that young children make of explanations in terms of simple natural laws. Thus he asked a child of 4 years and 5 months, 'How does this bicycle work?' The child replied, 'When you pedal'—a perfectly good general rule, telling us when the bicycle moves and when it does not (p. 200).

The rule is far from being a perfect one—bicycles move of their own accord when they go downhill. But the question was really designed to find out about the power source that drives the bicycle along and in these terms the answer is quite correct. When you pedal the bicycle is powered along, when you stop pedalling it stops being powered along. Piaget also asked the same child about a model steam engine in which the boiler was heated by a spirit lamp: 'What makes the wheel turn?' The child replied, 'When the thing (the lamp) is alight.' So bicycles move when you pedal and the steam engine goes when you light the lamp. These are both causal explanations in terms of natural laws. To say that they are 'social laws', 'imposed from outside', seems quite unnecessary.

More recent literature raises a number of further issues. Firstly, the question of the need for cause and effect to obey the temporal precedence principle, which states that a cause must appear shortly before or together with its effect (e.g. a gust of wind catches the sail and then the boat surges forward). A number of studies show that children as young as 3 years of age can rely on the temporal precedence principle and that under favourable conditions this will even outweigh their preference for spatial contact or nearness.[10] However, 3, 4 and 5 year olds' mastery of this principle is easily disrupted by distracting events that catch their attention and by their tendency to forget the premises for their arguments. In addition young children are hampered by inability to understand verbal questions and difficulties in framing their replies.

In looking at children's understanding of covariance principles one paradigm has been to show an effect E and two possible causes A and B. If the situation is that A causes E then on different occasions the child is shown A and B with E, A with E and B without E. Shultz and Mendelson (1975) found that while children of 9-11 years drew the correct inference more often than children from 3-4 years, even the younger children were able to make some use of the principle.

Other studies show that younger children will tend to judge any event A that often precedes another event E as the cause of E.[11] They do prefer a cause to precede its effect on 100 per cent of occasions but will be satisfied with much less than this.[12] This tendency to accept something that is often associated with something else as its cause is another example of the tendency for the young child's thinking to be dominated by associations. By 8 years children are already moving away from this to something more like explicit testing of a causal hypothesis.

Something close to Piaget's (1929, 1930) 'magical thinking' has been demonstrated in other studies of young children.[13] It has been found that children in the 4-7 age range are prone to using physical similarity between the cause A and an effect E even when this conflicts with principles of covariation. Older children progressively use covariation principles to override physical similarity.

More complex covariations between cause and effect have also been studied under the heading of 'causal schemas' (Kelley, 1972, 1973). Two principles are of particular interest. In the Graded Effects (GE) schema two causes (A, B) act to produce an effect (E). The more each cause increases in magnitude the more the effect increases. When both increase the effect is magnified even further. An example would be the effect of drought and a disease in producing poor crops.

This schema was originally investigated by Piaget who found that younger children tend to think the two causes interact by simple arithmetical addition, while adolescents are prepared to hypothesise that their effects interact by arithmetical multiplication (the effect (E) being directly proportional to the magnitude of A times the magnitude of B).[14] A more recent study found slightly earlier ages.[15]

While the effects of different kinds of content have not yet been fully explored it is fairly clear that young children begin to grasp some causal principles from as young as 3 years of age and that their improvement thereafter tends to be gradual rather than one involving a sudden leap.[16] This means that ideas about causality introduced in primary science classes should increase in complexity throughout the age range. Two ap-

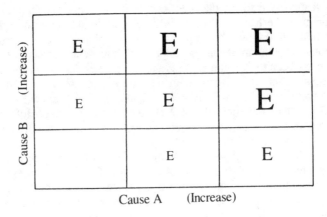

Fig. 1. *Graded Effects Schema*

parently simple schemas, however, remain particularly difficult for primary age children. One is Inhelder and Piaget's (1955) schema of 'all other things being equal'. This states that for independent factors we should investigate causality by maintaining all but one factor constant and varying the factor under examination. Thus in investigating if weight, length or amplitude of swing affect the rate of swing of a pendulum, we might keep weight and length constant and vary amplitude of swing to see if that has an effect on rate of swing. The other apparently simple idea that remains difficult for young children is that involved when the magnitude of effect is directly proportional to the product of the magnitude of the causes ($E = A \times B$). However, the study of Kun *et al.* (1974) shows that in familiar situations this kind of reasoning may be possible for the average child as young as 9 years of age. In addition, the more complex problem of devising experiments to test for causality where it is suspected that several causes are both necessary and sufficient for an effect remains difficult even in early adolescence.

While there have been many attempts to teach the more complex principle of 'all other things being equal', none seem to have been reported on the simpler causal schemas found in primary school. In devising methods for teaching elementary principles it seems likely that the Karplus learning cycle will be of help. We might consider teaching children from 8 or 9 years that 'A causes B' means 'If you find A then B must follow'. We could begin by setting up situations where this is true and where it is not. For instance, we could have the children fill up bottles with water. Each time some is poured in they have to say if the note obtained by tapping the bottle with a spoon goes up. (This is a case where A—pouring in water— causes B—rise in note). Next the children could take a dice and make a wish for it to come down on a number, throw it three times and see if it comes down on the number, then repeating the experiment by wishing another number. Sometimes the wish will come true and sometimes not. (This is a case where A—the wish—does not cause B—the number coming up within three throws). Following these experiments children could then be shown in a talk or demonstration that 'A causes B' means 'If you find A then B must follow'. Then the children could be asked to investigate more situations involving simple cause and effect relationships.

Before concluding this section something more should be said about one particular variety of causal thinking in young children which was prominent in the studies of Piaget (1929, 1930)—animism. Piaget (1929) devoted a whole section of his book to this topic. In one study he found that when asked such questions as 'If I were to prick the table (with a pin) would the table feel it?', young children up to 6 or 7 years tended to say that the inanimate object mentioned will feel pain. From 6-7 until 8-9 such consciousness is only imputed to objects that we normally think of as associated with movement, such as billiard balls, bicycles and watches. At the third stage (8-9 until 11-12) it is only those objects that move by themselves (such as watches) that are endowed with consciousness. It is not until 11-12 years of age that consciousness is attributed only to animals and human beings. In addition to the question about the pin, this sequence was backed up by replies about the thoughts and feelings of inanimate objects in other situations. In a second study children were asked whether or not various objects and animals were 'alive' or not and why. The results supported the stages just outlined in the sense that at first all kinds of inanimate objects were, on occasion, claimed to be alive; later only objects associated with movement, then objects moving of their own accord. Finally, the adult distinction is reached around 11-12 years of age.

An early study critical of Piaget's work here was that of Deutsche (1937), who found as a result of extensive interviews with children that animism did not appear with sufficient frequency among young children to be reliably scored. In addition, Deutsche found no evidence of sudden stage-like jumps in development, but rather a gradual increase in more mature types of causal explanation.

Deutsche's interviews were similar to Piaget's (1930) questions about a bicycle in that children were asked to explain phenomena demonstrated to them. Most of the phenomena were rather simpler than the mechanism of a bicycle or the model steam engine used by Piaget, though they sometimes involved the action of unseen influences, as when a candle was lit, a jar placed over it and then the child asked why the candle went out. This may explain some of the differences with Piaget's results.

From the teacher's point of view Deutsche's results are the more relevant as we would expect to begin teaching causality in simplified situations. More recent studies have also shown that familiar things are easier to judge as to whether they are alive or not.[17] We do find, however, that as children get older they develop a more sophisticated idea of what it is to be alive. Younger children tend to rely on whether something can move of its own accord to find out if it is alive. Even 7 and 8 year olds have difficulty in giving the biologist's criteria of need for nutriment, breathing and reproduction.[18]

There has often been speculation in the literature about the influence of parental teaching on children's animistic thinking. Recently Billingham and Fu (1980) were able to show that the extent of young children's animistic responses increased with the mother's tendency to produce animistic descriptions, but not with that of the father. This implies that if either as parents or as teachers we adopt the strategy of speaking animistically to young children 'so they can understand us', we are in danger of contributing to animistic tendencies.[19]

Turning to studies specifically related to teaching, Wolfinger (1982) found that 300 minutes of instruction about the differences between living and non-living things resulted in a significant reduction in both animism and dynamism in children from 4½-7 years, though there was evidence that developmental readiness for such instruction increased its impact, particularly on dynamism. Abdullah and Lowell (1981) also found that as age increased from 5-10 years, so did improvement resulting from instruction in the characteristics of 'animals' and 'insects'.[20]

Bell (1981) found that in considering whether such things as spiders and worms are animals the majority of 12 year olds favoured 'number of legs' as a criterion (usually saying animals have four legs), followed by 'It moves', 'It breathes', 'It has a brain', 'It lives on land'. Apart from movement none of these are characteristics used by biologists to define animals. It appeared that even junior secondary students tend to associate the term 'animal' with dogs, cats and farmyard animals, denying that insects and fish are animals. This confusion is probably chiefly one derived from the contexts in which they have heard the term 'animal' used rather than from inability to use the biological definitions when these are explained, although Wolfinger (1982) warned that many of his primary aged students tended readily to revert from the biological definition of 'alive' to everyday notions.[21]

CHILDREN'S PHYSICS

Gravity and Cosmography

Piaget (1930) reported an interview study of children's understanding of the movement of the heavenly bodies, particularly the sun and the moon.

He claimed that the same five stages in understanding these phenomena appeared between the ages of 4 and 12 as for other aspects of physical causation. In the first, up to around 5 years, the cause of movement is magical and animistic. For instance, the movement of the moon is explained by the movement of people and animals (explanation by magical similarity). In the second, from about 5-6, the movement is supervised by God or people. In the third stage, from about 6-8, clouds, night, rain and other natural phenomena are believed to be alive and to be responsible for movement, just as God and people were at the previous stage. Piaget also emphasises that up until the end of the third stage children take as much interest in the illusion they have that the moon follows them around at night as they do in the phases of the moon and its movements across the sky. This is an optical illusion arising from the fact that there are few cues to the real distance of the moon and it is imagined to be nearer than it is. If, for instance, the child walks down a street and sees the moon over the chimney of the first house it will apparently follow the child down the street and perch over each chimney in turn. If a near body like a balloon did this it would have to move to do so; the moon only appears to do so because of its great distance.

In the fourth stage, from about 8-9 years, children re-invent the Aristotelian idea that the motion of bodies like arrows or stones through the air is due to a 'reflux' of air displaced from the leading face of the moving object round to the back. Unlike Aristotle, children also apply this to the sun and moon. Also found at this stage are explanations based on the idea that wind as a natural force or vapour thrown off by the heavenly bodies moves them. At the fifth stage, from 9 years on, children still believe that the sun and moon are at about the same height as the clouds, but they now explain their motion by the action of wind or expelled vapour and are said to lose the last vestige of a moral approach to the problem. It is, however, rather difficult to detect the difference between stages 4 and 5 in the interviews reported in the book.

Some interviews previously reported in Piaget (1929) on the phases of the moon reinforce the general Piagetian contention that until 11 or 12 years children's conception of the behaviour of the heavenly bodies is quite rudimentary. Thus from 6-8 years the child thinks either that the moon, as a conscious agent, cuts itself up, or that the wind, again acting as a conscious agent, does so. Alternative explanations at this stage are based on the idea that the moon pivots on its axis thus displaying different faces or that it is obscured by clouds.

Nussbaum and Novak (1976) interviewed 7 year olds about their conceptions of the Earth. One group had received six lessons dealing with the earth, aeroplanes, gravity and force; the other received no such instruction. In both groups five different conceptions of the earth were detected. Notion 1 has it that the earth is flat and not round. Notion 2 recognises that the earth is a sphere and children holding this conception can often give proofs of this, such as the possibility of travelling around the globe or pictures taken from space. However, they lack an understanding of gravity and (being North American children) they think objects will fall off the earth in the southern hemisphere and that space is limited by a bottom and possibly sides. Notion 3 children realise that space is unlimited but still think objects fall off the earth in the southern hemisphere. Notion 4 children realise that objects don't fall off the earth in the southern hemisphere, but are still uncertain about precisely which direction they will fall. Thus if offered the two diagrams in Figure 2 as representing a cross-section of the earth with deep holes or mineshafts dug in it, these children will often pick holes N and K as the holes down which objects will fall as they relate up-down to up-down on the paper, rather than to the centre of the earth.

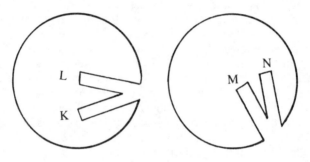

Fig. 2. *Diagrams of the Earth*

Notion 5 children understand 1) that earth is a spherical planet, 2) that it is surrounded by limitless space, and 3) that things fall towards its centre.

If we consider only students at Notions 3, 4 and 5 a greater percentage of the instructed than of the uninstructed students were at Notions 4 or 5 than at Notion 3. The same proportion of the two groups were at Notion 1 and Notion 2. This is consistent with the view that children at Notions 1 and 2 are not yet ready to profit from instruction, while those at Notions 3 and 4 are. In addition a majority of both groups of these 7 year old children were at Notion 3 or above, which contradicts Piaget's claim that 7 year olds have only a very hazy grasp of cosmography.[22]

Floating and Sinking

Inhelder and Piaget (1955) report a series of stages in understanding why some bodies float in water and others sink. Children were shown various objects made of wood and metal, shown some demonstrations of floating and sinking, and asked to say why some objects float and others sink. From about 5-8 years children simply pick on one aspect of a given comparison to explain matters. Thus if a big object like a block of wood is shown to float and a small one like a pin to sink, they will say 'Big ones float'. When shown that a large metal object sinks they may say 'Because it's metal' or 'Because it's square', showing no embarrassment at thus contradicting their original statement. From about 8-12 years children show some awareness of the problem of explaining why some large objects float and others sink and produce replies based on an intuitive, non-quantitative notion of density. Only from 13 years on will density be correctly understood as weight per unit volume.

Novak (1977) criticised Piaget's interpretation of these results, arguing that they can be interpreted within non-Piagetian theories such as that of Ausubel (1963, 1968) which emphasises a gradual differentiation and then further re-integration of concepts within specific domains rather than the generalised stages of Piaget. Indeed, Inhelder and Piaget's (1955) scale for concepts of floating and sinking can be largely explained as the product of logical necessity. It is logically impossible for a child to understand weight per unit volume quantitatively without understanding it intuitively. It is also impossible to understand weight per unit volume without understanding weight and volume. We know from a variety of studies that conservation of weight appears around 9 years or later and conservation of volume around 12 years or even later (Modgil and Modgil, 1976b). Thus it is not surprising to find that the conception of ratio between weight and volume appears later than this. Bearison (1975) has suggested that achievement of weight and volume conservation is a necessary state of 'readiness' for being taught about floating and sinking.

Heat, Work and Energy

Piaget, first on the scene as ever, undertook a number of studies of heat, work and energy. Piaget (1929) reports interviews with children about the origins of snow. Up to about 7 years, he found answers dominated by artificialism: snow is made by God or by people who manufacture it in the sky. From about 7-9 naturalistic explanations begin, but snow is thought to originate from something other than water; often it is said to be 'bits of sky' or formed from air. Finally, after about 9 years, it is understood that snow is formed from water. The role of the cold in being associated with snow is understood from early on, but at first this is a superficial phenomenistic or magical connection. In addition, children up to 7 years often think that 'cold' is 'the air', an idea presumably derived from the feeling of cold we get when a cold wind blows. From 7 years on children come to a more accurate idea of cold and this is held to cause ice and, somewhat later, snow.

Piaget (1971) reports more elaborate investigations of the concept of heat. In one study a steel ball is heated in the presence of the child and then plunged into cold water or a cold ball plunged into hot water. In both cases the child is shown the change in temperature of the ball and asked to explain it. Under about 7 years children did not admit that heat was transferred from the ball to the liquid or from the liquid to the ball. One-third of 6 year olds admitted that the hot ball would heat the water but would not admit that the ball would cool down. Between about 7 and 11 children admit there is an exchange of heat from ball to water or vice versa but do not affirm the conservation of heat in the transfer. This is only admitted by a majority after 11 years. A number of other experiments were claimed to show that though from 7 years children admit the transmission of heat between two bodies in physical contact, it is only at 11 years that the conduction of heat through an intermediate solid or liquid or by radiation through the atmosphere is admitted.

Albert (1978) reported an extensive series of interviews about heat with young children. He concluded that up to around 6 years we find the child thinks of some bodies as hot like a fire or the sun because they warm the child's body. Even at this early stage there is, contrary to Piaget's claims, an understanding of heat radiating from such sources based on personal experience. From about 5 or 6 years, the child views such radiation from a less egocentric viewpoint and realises that the sun and fires warm inanimate objects subjected to radiant heat. In addition children up to 5 or 6 years tend to think that when an electrical heater or oven is switched on it becomes hot immediately, but after this age it is realised that a gradual process of becoming hot intervenes. At about 8 years children come to think of heat as a dimension with several grades (warm, very warm, hot, etc.). They also have a clearer idea about the movement of heat in space, particularly in relation to the convection of heat in the atmosphere. The conception of heat as a dimension is broadened to include temperature measured in degrees which is helped by reading thermometers. Around 8 or 9 years children also come to realise that mechanical energy can be translated into heat as they are familiar with friction burns on their skin and the heating up of bearings and other moving surfaces.

Stavy et al. (1974) reported on a study that attempted to teach the concept of temperature to 9 year olds. Children measured the temperature of water in two containers, both at 10°C. They then poured the two containers into a larger vessel. Many children thought the temperature of water in the larger vessel would be 20°C and even when shown that the new temperature was 10°C many attributed this to a broken thermometer.

Strauss et al. (1977) reported studies of a number of heat-related ideas, of which the following four are samples.

One study involved quantitative assessment of the temperature of mixtures of liquids of equal temperatures as just described. Between 8 and 11 years there was a systematic rise in the success rate, and at 11 it had reached 85 per cent. A qualitative version of the mixture of equal temperatures where the temperature of the initial two vessels was judged by hand as cold, warm or hot, showed that 70 per cent of 4 year olds succeeded, 25 per cent of 6 year olds and 85 per cent of 11 year olds. Two corresponding studies were reported of children's predictions about mixtures of liquids from vessels at unequal temperatures. By 6 years all children could predict the qualitative version, while the quantitative version was found difficult, even at age 11.

The above trends show that many children are able to give correct judgements when qualitative assessments like cold, warm and hot are given, but they go wrong when the same problem is given with numerical temperatures. Stavy and Berkowitz (1980) successfully exploited this conflict by bringing it to the children's attention when they made conflicting judgements on successive tests. Their success here does not, however, show that training by conflict is superior to training by other methods, such as direct confrontation with the measured temperature of the two liquids when mixed, as their control group had no training at all.

Piaget (1971) looked at the idea of work by showing children a four-step stairway and a number of equal weights. He asked how many weights would a crane have to carry up the first step to perform an amount of work equal to the work done in lifting one weight to the fourth step. Until about 7 years the amount of work done was judged by the height of the lift alone or by the number of weights lifted alone but not by both. From 7-11 years there are intuitive attempts to say that if we have greater height we need to lift less weights, but, as in attempts to state the law of floating bodies, realisation that there is the precise numerical relationship specified by the function 'work = force × distance' does not appear in most children until after 11 years. This conclusion was backed up by a number of other studies of typically Piagetian ingenuity.

A study by Osborne and Gilbert (1980) touches briefly on the concept of work in children from 7-11. As we might expect, children in this age range in the absence of specific instruction tend to think of work in the everyday sense of 'effort expended by the human body'. They will, for instance, claim that a person pushing on a car that doesn't move is doing work, though in terms of the physics definition no work is done as the force is not being applied over distance.

The concept of energy when defined in quantitative terms is outside the capacity of most primary age children. However, Urevbu (1984) has shown that even 7 year old children can achieve a fairly detailed descriptive understanding of energy, particularly when this forms part of their curriculum. An example of such descriptive understanding was that in reply to the question 'Would you say petrol has energy?', a child might say 'Yes. Car engines burn petrol, turning chemical energy into heat.'

While we would not expect the use of the technical phrase 'turning chemical energy into heat' in children who had no explicit teaching on this subject, it was found among those who had. Urevbu (1984) also describes a 'descriptive' level of teaching strategy suitable for the younger child. Thus:

> This lesson gives children the opportunity to recognise descriptive energy concepts with their own personal sensation. Energy is introduced as a "quality" present or absent in man as well as objects or things and which can be felt in a sensorimotor way . . . The teacher gives the child a list of familiar objects asking about each in turn, "Does it have energy?", "Why does it possess energy?" The order of this list is roughly as follows: a man, a dog, a fish, a fly, a pebble, the sun, fire, wind, a car, etc.

The notion of forms of energy is taught descriptively by using 'carefully chosen examples of the different forms of energy to identify heat, sound, mechanical and electrical energy, which are illustrated through activities and drawings.'

Urevbu (1984) also makes a useful distinction between 'comparative' concepts suitable for somewhat older primary children and 'quantitative' concepts of energy suitable only for children in secondary school. An example of a 'comparative' energy concept is when a child is asked 'Why do different people need different amounts of food?', and the child replies, 'The amount of food depends on how active we are.' Here there is a qualitative concept of 'more' and 'less' but no precise quantification. An example of comparative teaching is 'The teacher displays a variety of food items for children to see and touch. The children are taught to compare foods which provide the most energy per 100 gm, foods which provide the least energy . . .'

A questionnaire survey of American fourth grade children on energy issues by Lawrenz (1983) also bears out Urevbu's contention that even without teaching older primary age children pick up a fair amount of information about energy. For instance, 74 per cent knew enough to contradict the assertion that 'heavier cars use less gasoline than lighter cars', and 56 per cent knew enough to contradict 'solar collectors make pollution'. Some of the questions were found difficult, but these were chiefly on matters of information that high school students also had difficulty with.[23]

Electricity

Piaget never seems to have conducted a systematic study of children's conception of an electric current, but he does assert in an aside in one of his books that electric current being invisible and therefore non-concrete is not understood by children until around 11 years of age (Piaget, 1971, p.

28). As we shall see this claim is quite incorrect. (This, incidentally, is an example of Piaget himself interpreting the term 'concrete operations' in the misleading way criticised in the Introduction.)

Osborne and Gilbert (1980) interviewed a number of students in the range 7-11 years about the current in a circuit comprising an electric light connected to a battery. Many students in the younger part of this age range knew that electrons went along the wires to make the lamp light up, but they were unaware that current passes through the battery as well as the bulb. This misconception persisted in some students into late adolescence. Koslowski *et al.* (1981) found even 4 and 5 year olds use explanations based on comparing electric current with water or other fluids.

In more detailed studies Osborne (1982, 1983) confronted children with a battery with a wire attached to each terminal and a light bulb with a wire attached to each of its connections. When given this apparatus only six pupils in the age range 8-12 years connected the circuit up correctly. Twenty-two connected only one terminal of the battery to one (or sometimes two) of the connections on the bulb. Eleven shorted out the battery and placed the bulb somewhere convenient. Thus most students imagined it sufficient to have current going out to the bulb without any provision for it to return to the battery. Many others seemed just confused. There appeared to be little age trend in the success level and all successful students were boys rather than girls. These facts suggest that the failure of many of the children was due to lack of specific information about the topic. On being given a correct model all children successfully copied it. Following this the children were asked in which direction the current went. The majority said it went out from each terminal of the battery and along the wires to the bulb. On being forced to abandon their original model of current flowing out from one terminal owing to the lack of success of circuits set up like this, students had now assimilated the new double connections to their old theory that currents go from battery to bulb but not back. Further discussions of their models of current failed to change the majority of students' ideas, though a few did so.

Osborne *et al.* (1981) had previously found that although it was, as in the later study, relatively easy to alter children's 'one wire flowing from battery to bulb' idea to 'two wires flowing from battery to bulb' in a simple circuit, if something less visible (like a flashlight) or more complicated was introduced students readily relapsed to the one-wire theory.

Overall these results are not encouraging for teaching electric current in the primary school. However, Osborne (1983) is right to advise further efforts in this direction, provided they are directed at the direction of flow of currents and not at quantitative studies of electrical energy and the laws of electrical transmission. Once a child has grasped that there is something invisible in the wires, which most upper primary graders do know, the business of explaining how current goes around simple circuits is only adding slightly more complexity, rather than setting out to teach an entirely new concept.

Atoms and Molecules

Piaget and Inhelder (1941) conducted a study in which sugar is dissolved in water and the child asked where the sugar has gone. From about 7 years children begin to suggest that the sugar is composed of tiny particles, to which some of them give the name 'atoms', which float around in the water though they are too small to see. Such children will also assert that if all the water were to evaporate the sugar would come back again and there would remain the same amount as at the start.

Piaget (1971) also asked children about the difference between solid objects like a stone, powders like flour and liquids like water and oil. Even before 7 years children often appeal to a primitive atomic theory in explaining why water and powders can be poured and will alter their shape depending on the vessel, while stones will not. They say that the liquids contain little pieces that are 'all broken up' and so they are pourable. In solids the little pieces are 'tight' and well stuck together. After about 7 years this idea becomes more differentiated and is used to explain both why some liquids like molasses flow more slowly and why when powders like flour are wetted they become sticky and less pourable. These things are now explained as being due to the invisible particles sticking more firmly together.

Piaget (1971) also reviews his earlier studies of children's understanding of states of matter, as when ice becomes water and then steam. Here again he finds the same evolution. Up to about 7 years changes in states of matter are often explained by the sticking together or ungluing of little particles. After about 7 years the conservation of matter is asserted when freezing, melting, evaporation and condensation are observed, as it is felt there must be the same number of little particles after as before. At about 11 years the idea takes root that the particles in a liquid are moving about all the time, while in a solid they stay still. Piaget points out that changes in the states of unfamiliar substances and conceptions of invisible gases lag somewhat behind more familiar and visible instances. The transformation of water into ice is a particularly easily understood case.

Piaget's writings about young children's conceptions of the atomic constitution of matter would lead us to think that children in the upper primary years already have the basis for instruction about the atomic theory of matter. Furthermore, there should be little difficulty in their absorbing large-scale models of atoms and molecules and then equating these with their intuitive ideas about the 'tiny particles' that constitute matter. Battino (1983) has reported a project to teach the atomic theory of matter in the upper primary school focusing on a particular set of apparatus used to build molecular models. While no formal evaluation was made, the overall impression given was that the teachers involved in the project found no undue difficulties in teaching atomic theory with concrete apparatus at this level. In agreement with this Comber (1983) replicated Piaget and Inhelder's test for the conservation of dissolving sugar on a large sample. When the results of this and a number of interview items relating to atomic theory were compared with the teaching practices of British primary school teachers it appeared that teaching on this topic was being unnecessarily delayed.[24]

CONCLUSIONS

Piaget and his collaborators underestimated the abilities of the younger child in regard to both classification and causality. This underestimation has more serious implications for the teacher in relation to causality. Simple forms of causal explanation can be introduced right from the start of the primary years. Piaget also underestimated children's mental models for physical processes. It is now believed that qualitative or comparative explanations of cosmography, heat, work, energy, electric current and atomic structure can readily be introduced in the upper grades of the primary school. In teaching physics concepts and models at all levels in the primary school attention should be paid to providing both practical experience and an explicit statement of the principle or picture of the model. Often this can be most readily achieved through Karplus's learning cycle of exploration, concept introduction and application.

FURTHER READING

Inhelder and Piaget (1964) is still essential reading on classification concepts; Sugarman (1983), Markman (1983) and Medin (1983) provide useful surveys of more recent material. Piaget (1929, 1930) should be read critically on early concepts of causation; Bullock *et al.* (1982), Gelman *et al.* (1983), Bullock (1985a,b) and Shultz *et al.* (1986) provide useful surveys of more recent work. On gravity and cosmography see Piaget (1930) and Nussbaum and Novak (1976); on floating and sinking see Inhelder and Piaget (1955) and Novak (1977); on heat, work and energy see Piaget (1971), Albert (1978) and Urevbu (1984); on electricity see Osborne *et al.* (1981), Osborne (1982, 1983), Osborne and Freyberg (1985); on atoms and molecules see Piaget (1971), Stavy and Stachel (1985) and Comber (1983, 1985). An English translation of Piaget (1971) appeared in 1974 under the title *Understanding Causality*, Norton, New York.

NOTES

1. For a review see Langford and Berrie (1974).
2. The line of argument developed below does not dispute Inhelder and Piaget's observations in their original testing situation. Although Brainerd (1978a) doubts that graphic collections appear even here, this has not been claimed by other investigators; a detailed refutation of Brainerd's claim is given by Vincenzo and Kelly (1984).
3. Kemler and Smith (1978), Smith (1979), Carbonnel (1982), Smith and Kemler (1977, 1978), Kemler (1982), Mervis and Crisafi (1982). On natural categories more generally see Rosch *et al.* (1976), Tversky (1977), Rosch (1978). The natural categories view has been extended to class inclusion problems by Markman (1978, 1979), Markman and Siebert (1976), Markman *et al.* (1980), Horton and Markman (1980), Markman (1983). Sugarman (1983) makes related but slightly different claims about early classification. The views of Kendler and Kendler (1962, 1975), based on discrimination learning, are similar to those of Inhelder and Piaget in that they emphasise the tendency in middle childhood to begin to try to solve classification problems by using dimensions, though they put the onset of this slightly later than Inhelder and Piaget. Kendler and Guenther (1980) and Kendler (1983) have tried to expand their earlier ideas about dimension use to explain early category use but in my view this is unsuccessful. In particular they claim there is a tendency for category width to narrow during early childhood, while the empirical literature is quite equivocal on this: Saltz *et al.* (1972), Neimark (1974), Rosch (1973), Nelson (1974), Anglin (1977), Nelson *et al.* (1978). For a recent study of the influence of task difficulty on classification see Markman *et al.* (1981). Note, however, that Markman *et al.*'s task is unlikely to be encountered in classroom situations.
4. See Posner and Keele (1968), Rosch *et al.* (1976), Medin and Schaffer (1978), Hintzman and Ludlum (1980), Medin and Smith (1981), Medin (1983).
5. The former effect is also demonstrated in Saxby and Anglin (1983).
6. See Brainerd and Kaszor (1974) and Kofsky (1966).
7. See Modgil and Modgil (1976a) and Winer (1980).
8. Rosenthal and Zimmerman (1978), Brainerd (1978a), Kuhn (1972), Rosser and Horan (1982), Lawton and Wanska (1979), Sugimura (1978), Sato (1978), Ryman (1977).
9. See Ammon (1981), Koslowski *et al.* (1981).

10. Kuhn and Phelps (1976), Corrigan (1975), Shultz and Mendelson (1975), Kun (1978), Bullock and Gelman (1979), Bullock *et al.* (1982), Sophian and Huber (1984), Bullock (1985a,b).
11. For other studies of covariance see Siegler (1975), (1976), Siegler and Liebert (1974).
12. Shultz and Mendelson (1975), Shaklee and Paszek (1985). On selection of causal rules see Shultz *et al.* (1986).
13. Huang *et al.* (1945), Shultz and Ravinsky (1977).
14. Inhelder and Piaget (1955), Piaget *et al.* (1968).
15. Kun *et al.* (1974). See also Kun (1977).
16. See Bullock *et al.* (1982), Bullock (1985a).
17. Nass (1956), Berzonsky (1971, 1974), Looft and Bartz (1969), Looft and Charles (1969), Looft (1973, 1974). Recent studies also show a gradual increase in the number of criteria used to define 'living' with age: Holland and Rohrman (1979), Williamson (1981), Beveridge and Davies (1983), Lucas *et al.* (1979).
18. See Bullock (1985a,b), Gelman *et al.* (1983), Tunmer (1985).
19. See also Sharp *et al.* (1985).
20. See also Sedgwick *et al.* (1978).
21. See also Trowbridge and Mintzes (1985). Brumby (1982) found reversion to prescientific definitions was common even in tertiary biology students outside an academic context.
22. The Nussbaum and Novak (1976) study has been refined and replicated by Nussbaum (1979), Mali and Howe (1979), Klein (1982), Nussbaum and Sharoni-Dagan (1983) and Sneider and Pulos (1983). The sequence of development occurs more slowly in some countries (e.g. Nepal) than in North America. Za'rour (1976) has reported a study of concepts of the moon and clouds.
23. See also Lawrentz and Dantchek (1986).
24. Beveridge (1985) has shown the relative ineffectiveness of such instruction earlier on in the primary school, while Comber (1985) thinks 8 or 9 a suitable time to start.

Chapter 6

MATHEMATICS

INTRODUCTION

This chapter will be limited chiefly to the development of children's understanding and use of arithmetic. Before embarking on this topic, one or two remarks about the teaching of both geometry and Boolean logic (set theory) will be in order.

According to Piaget *et al.* (1960) the development of a 'real' grasp of angles must wait upon the understanding of how to co-ordinate spatial dimensions, which does not occur until towards the end of primary school. This belief is based largely upon special pleading and the unusual way in which they assess the concept of angle. If we revert to the conventional method, which would be to ask children to measure angles and use the result, then there is no doubt that most children of 8 or 9 years can understand angles. Thus there is really no theoretical reason why some simple geometry should not be taught at primary level.[1] Practical experience shows that it is possible to do so.

The teaching of set theory to primary school children was one of the features of the 'new maths' that became popular in the United States in the 1960s. Efforts were also made to teach set theory in primary school in other countries. Such efforts seem to have stemmed from two rather disparate sources. On the one hand some mathematicians believe that set theory provides an overall framework for understanding other branches of mathematics. This is a very misleading view as the kind of set theory used in mathematics to deal, for instance, with geometry involves infinite sets, which are not understood by most secondary schoolchildren (Langford, 1974; Fischbein *et al.*, 1979). On the other hand, Piaget argued that the logic concepts of the 'grouping structures' must precede understanding of number (Piaget, 1941, 1963, 1967). This was actually a rather different claim from that implemented in the new maths as the grouping structures form only a fragment of Boolean logic. It nonetheless fed into a rather generalised belief that if children learned about set theory this would benefit their understanding of number and arithmetic. This belief has been widely criticised by neo-Piagetian writers.[2] One objection is that to attempt to define arithmetical operations through operations on sets is both unnatural and unnecessary.[3] Another is that understanding of the laws of Boolean logic occurs consistently later than understanding of the corresponding laws in arithmetic (Langford, 1981).

CONSERVATION

Piaget (1941) used a demonstration in which he filled two identical containers with water to the same level. He then poured water from one of the two containers into several smaller but equal ones. Sometimes the liquid was then poured from one of the smaller containers into two even smaller containers. At the first stage he found that most children used either the level of water ('less') or the number of containers ('more') as the rule determining whether there was less or more after the pouring. Often the two rules were used successively by the same child. In addition, some children sometimes used size of container as the basis for judgement, while the relative fullness or emptiness of the container was used by others.

At stage 2 we have children who maintain conservation when the differences in level are slight or the liquid is poured into only two containers but fail to do so when the difference in levels or number of containers is greater. It appears they are able to resist perceptual suggestion when it is slight but not when it is great. Finally at stage 3 children maintain conservation through all transformations. Piaget claims that 'stage' 2 is 'not necessarily found in all children', though as his study was cross-sectional it is hard to see how he knew this.

Later on in the book Piaget looked at the conservation of one-to-one correspondence. Six little bottles and six little glasses on a tray were put on the table in front of the child. The experimenter then says, 'Look at these little bottles. What shall we need if we want to drink?' The child is asked to take enough glasses from the tray so there is one for each bottle. At stage 1 the child does not succeed. At stage 2 children succeed in establishing correspondence between the bottles and glasses by placing every glass next to or opposite a bottle. If the bottles were then placed in a long row with the glasses next to them the child would still believe there was the same number of each. But remove the glasses and place them in a small group and the same child would say there are more bottles because they appear to be more. At stage 3, which later studies have placed at around 6½ years for the average child, equality is asserted even when the glasses are grouped together in a small group (Modgil and Modgil, 1976, Part One).

There have perhaps been more studies of conservation learning than of any other concept and it would be quite impractical even to review the more recent ones in detail. Fortunately there are two very incisive recent reviews of this literature by Acredolo (1981, 1982) to which the reader may be referred for further information. What follows is an outline of some of the main lines of argument in the area and of their educational implications.

Piaget and his co-workers for many years maintained that the three kinds of arguments that children give to justify their answers when they give a correct conservation judgement are the key to understanding how children learn conservation. These are known as the identity, compensation and reversibility arguments. The identity argument says that the amount or number remains unchanged because nothing has been added and nothing taken away. The compensation argument justifies conservation by saying that although one dimension gets bigger another gets smaller. In the correspondence experiment this takes the form of arguing that although objects spread out in a line look more if you judge by the length of line, this is compensated for by the large size of the gaps between them. The reversibility argument justifies conservation by saying that you can return the objects or liquid that have been spread out or poured into a different container to their original arrangement or container.

This reversibility argument suited Piaget's theoretical purposes because he put so much emphasis on the general role of reversible operations in thought. To the unbiased observer the argument is, however, very peculiar as an explanation for learning as it is wrong. While some reversible operations are quantity-conserving, like changes of shape for liquid and changes of arrangement for objects, others are not. Adding and subtracting objects from a collection or heating up the mercury in a thermometer are both reversible operations, but the number of objects and the volume of mercury is changed by them. For this reason many people have been sceptical that children really use the reversibility argument as anything more than a spur of the moment justification for a judgement that is learned by other means.

There are also difficulties in assuming that children learn positive understanding by compensation as this really only tells us not to be misled by the change of dimensions. It is most unlikely that children actually know that when the length of a row of objects is increased by 10 centimetres then exactly 10 centimetres of extra length appears in the gaps, and even more unlikely that they can estimate the volume of liquids by looking at height and width.

This leaves identity as the only convincing positive argument, but it is one that assumes we already know what adding something on and what taking something away are. The problem faced by younger children is precisely that they think that pouring liquid from one container to another may add something on. How do they learn that this is not so?

Two basic arguments have been given to explain this. According to Gibson (1969) the difficulty is really simply in learning not to be misled and in paying attention to what perception already tells us. Gibson claims that conservation is already given in perception and all the child has to do is get clear about it. This kind of argument is, I think, most convincing in relation to the process of spacing out a row of objects. As each object in the row is moved we have a real sense that the process of moving the object is 'obviously' leaving the number of objects unchanged. It is when the child surveys the end result of such individual movements, so this argument goes, that it is misled. In line with this kind of claim Bruner (1966) and Bryant (1974) showed that if the misleading perceptual cues given by the changes in level of water and arrangement of objects were removed by screening them from the child or other means then conservation occurs somewhat earlier than Piaget had found. Even more striking were the studies of Gelman (1972) showing that children as young as 3 years appear able to conserve for small numbers of objects, though as Acredolo (1982) points out there is some doubt as to whether these studies really show conservation.[4]

The second argument is that young children of 3 and 4 years of age learn something about conservation of small numbers from subitising. This is the process by which we directly see the number of objects in a small collection. If the reader has someone set out from two to five objects on a table and cover them from sight with a book the essentials of this process can be appreciated. If the book is removed to show the objects for about a second you will be able to tell the number of objects without counting. It 'jumps out' at you.

The subitising theory suggests that by seeing small groups of objects being re-arranged in space the young child comes to realise that for small groups re-arrangement in space makes no difference. By first subitising the number when in arrangement A and then when in arrangement B the child is able to check that this is so (Klahr and Wallace, 1976).

This process works for small numbers, but it breaks down for numbers above five. For such numbers many researchers now believe the child must check that re-arrangement of objects makes no difference by counting first in arrangement A and then in arrangement B. The implication of this for the classroom teacher is that having children count objects following re-arrangement is likely to lead to conservation learning. Lifschitz and Langford (1977) found that teaching equality by counting led to greater and more permanent learning than simply telling children that the two amounts were the same.

So far matters are fairly clear. The point at which all the explanations outlined so far break down is, however, in dealing with conservation of continuous quantity, as in the water jars experiment. While some experimenters have successfully taught conservation of continuous quantity using a small dipper to measure out the liquid before and after transformation (e.g. Lifschitz and Langford, 1977), there is little likelihood that this occurs much in everyday life. The Gibson (1969) explanation is also much less plausible in this instance. It is quite easy to think that the perceptual apparatus can keep track of a number of objects being re-arranged as usually only one or two are moved at a time. It is much less easy to believe perception can keep track of the complex transformations of shape that occur when liquid is poured from one vessel to another. One possibility is that the child learns the identity rule from situations involving discontinuous quantity (collections of objects) and then transfers it to situations of continuous quantity (like liquids and plasticene).

NUMBER CONCEPTS

We have already seen that young children tend to be confused as to the effects of re-arrangements upon the number of objects in a collection. We can also ask what they actually mean in the first place by saying there are four or seven objects in a collection. This is usually referred to as their number concept.

There are four main theories about this in the psychological literature, some derived from older writings of philosophers and mathematicians, others of more recent origin. These theories differ both as to what young children mean when they announce the result of counting and as to what, if any, intuition children have about numbers before they learn to count. It is natural to think that in interpreting the meaning of counting young children feed off earlier ideas they have derived from experience, especially from perception. If someone said to an adult, 'I met a man from Mars yesterday', it would be natural for us to search around in our memory for pictures and descriptions of men from Mars so as to imagine what this man from Mars could have been like. The number names are initially just as mysterious for a young child as the expression 'man from Mars' is for an adult and young children possibly try to relate them to something they are already familiar with before learning to count. It may, of course, be true, as one of the theories alleges, that the child does not attempt this or fails, interpreting number names simply as 'what you get by counting in the approved manner'.

There are two kinds of meaning that children eventually learn to give to numbers. The cardinal number of a collection is that property it shares with all other collections of the same numerical size. Thus 'fiveness' belongs to a collection of five apples, five oranges, five motor cars, five trees or five buildings. The ordinal number of an object in a collection is the quality that belongs to it by being fifth or tenth in a series. Some confusion exists about just how we are to understand series here. In what we might call a natural series there is some property that can be used to order the objects without our having to count them. Thus a group of four people could be stood up against a wall with the shortest on the left and the tallest on the right. The third largest can then be established by counting down from the largest. Theorists like Brainerd (1973a,b, 1979) who argue that children begin from an ordinal concept of number say that the 'thirdness' of this member of the series stands out in perception. We know which is the third largest just by looking. This is probably possible for small numbers but seems unlikely for large ones.

In a counted series, on the other hand, we find the fourth or the seventh by counting. We might, for instance, want to know the tenth car passing a point or the sixth circle in a row of identical circles. Here there is no natural property that can be used to order the objects and we find out the tenth or sixth by counting. It is likely that an adult could still judge positions in a small series of identical objects all presented together by direct perception. Thus in a row of five circles we would be able to pick out the second from the left, or fourth from the left, just by looking.

The first of our four views of early number concepts is that of Piaget (1941). According to Piaget, children learn about the cardinal and ordinal properties of numbers at roughly the same time. However, as Brainerd (1979, p. 111) points out there is virtually no direct evidence presented in this book as to the interpretation that young children actually give to numbers, although some indirect evidence is given which I return to later. In general, however, Piaget simply assumes that young children could not possibly have a 'real' understanding of number until they know about the properties both of ordinal series and of cardination. He claims that these two things appear together, but his evidence for this is lacking in statistical detail. More importantly, he assesses the presence or absence of understanding ordination and cardination in ways that have since attracted much criticism.[5]

A second view of early number concepts has it that the concept of number is derived from the direct perception of small numbers by subitising.[6] When the child sees two objects or four objects together this twoness or fourness jumps out at them. When they learn to count they assume that the words 'two' and 'four' mean this seen twoness and fourness. This is gradually extended to larger numbers by analogy. This understanding of cardinal number is held to precede understanding of ordinal number, that is, of second or fourth. In defence of this we may cite the fact that young children typically learn to count collections of similar objects, not series of objects, and this is reinforced by their wall charts showing 'three apples' or 'five bananas' and many of their counting rhymes.

A third view, advanced by Brainerd (1973a,b), claims that ordinal number appears prior to cardinal number. One objection to much of Brainerd's work is that he persists in using Piagetian tests which have been widely criticised. He does, however, depart from this in some of the tests described in Brainerd (1979, pp. 169-73). Here he asked children to point out the meaning of numerals in relation either to a series of shapes (say, different sized triangles) or in relation to small collections of the same shape arranged like the numbers on a dice. He found that preschool children performed at the outset very similarly on these two tasks, which would seem to provide evidence against his theory, though he does not mention this. Brainerd was more interested in showing that it was easier to train children to associate the ordinal meaning with number names than the cardinal meaning, which he successfully achieved. There must, however, remain considerable doubt as to the implications of this finding. The greater ease in training the ordinal task may have been due more to the strategies the children used to solve his problems than to the meanings they attached to number names. We know that counting along a row of shapes is likely to be easier than counting a group of objects not arranged in a row; this would explain why it was easier to learn to count the series of shapes in a row than the groups of objects. Arranging a collection of objects like beans or buttons in a row in order to count them is one of the first strategies that children use in learning to count. Kingma and Koops (1981) have repeated some of Brainerd's studies in this area and while they were able to replicate his findings they share some of the reservations about his tasks rehearsed above. Michie (1985), using tasks more likely to index ordinal and cardinal number, found cardinal concepts develop first.

Finally we come to the fourth view of early number concepts, which has been most enthusiastically promoted by Gelman and Gallistel (1978). This says that young children initially think of numbers simply as 'what happens when you count'. We can distinguish a weak and a strong version of this view. The weak version would say that children adopt this view when they learn to count groups of objects, usually between 4 and 5 years of age. Prior to this age they have some other view of number, perhaps based on direct perception of cardinal number by subitising.

This weak view can draw much support from the fact that when children between five and six are asked how many objects or the number of objects in a collection they will usually count to find out. In Piaget's (1941) experiments on conservation of correspondence he already points out that once correspondence has been established and the experimenter then groups some objects together or extends a line of objects the initial reaction of many children in this age range when asked, 'Is there still the same number?' is to count to find out.

Gelman and Gallistel (1978) want to promote a stronger view which asserts that between the ages of 2 and 5 the use of counting has already become the preferred means for estimating the size of small groups of objects and that if subitising is ever a forerunner of counting as a means of estimating number this must occur before age 2 (p. 72). Their chief evidence for this is the observation that in their own experiments as well as in everyday life children in this age range persistently prefer to use counting to find out how many.[7] The difference between this and the weak view is, of course, a matter of degree and we might be on safer ground if we put reliance on counting at age 4 in the average child. This is not, however, a difference that has great educational significance.

In summary, the most popular views of early interpretations of number names base them either on the subitising of cardinal number or on the counting procedure. The strongest reason for concluding this is that young children normally learn counting by counting similar objects rather than by counting off objects in a series. It might seem unlikely therefore that they come to associate counting with anything other than either a perceptual intuition of cardinal properties or simply the procedure of counting itself. Brainerd (1979) showed, however, that children seemed able to tell the ordinal position of an object in a series at roughly the same age as they could tell the number of objects in a collection. He calls these tests of ordinal and cardinal number but this seems to be rather an adult-centered way of considering them. It is quite likely that the children actually used silent counting to solve his tasks. In this case the problem would be to know what they thought the result of their counting actually meant. It may well be that children do count objects in a counting series often enough to attach some kind of ordinal meaning to the result of counting. While children don't have much experience of counting objects arranged in a natural series (e.g. objects arranged in order of size) they have a lot more of counting objects arranged in a counting series. Examples of this kind of experience would be finding a numbered coat peg in the kindergarten or counting off moves along the board in a dice game. This would lead us back to a much altered version of Piaget's claim that intuitions of cardinal number and of ordinal number appear at about the same time. Brainerd's (1979) study shows that children certainly seem to be able to find 'number 6' in a series at around the same time as they can find 'the collection with 6 objects in it'. I suspect that they really understand 'number 6' in the series primarily as a counting order rather than as 'the sixth tallest', as Brainerd thinks. Children may well begin at a very early age from a perceptual notion of cardinal number based on subitising, but Brainerd's study shows that children between 4 and 5 years of age can already find the cardinal number of a set and the ordinal position in a series with about equal facility. As this is the state they achieve immediately prior to primary school this seems the most educationally significant result. Counting for both ordinal and cardinal number should thus be introduced in the final year of preschool rather than delayed, as Piagetians used to argue, until the age of about 6½ years when children understand conservation of correspondence.[8]

An issue that is considerably less clear is what we should do to help the child's transition from a counting view of number to a more advanced one.

If young children initially think of number as 'the answer you get by counting' then there must come a point at which they move away from this to think about cardinal and ordinal number, that is about 'threeness' and 'the fifth one'. In one sense they must be able to do this at a relatively early age or they wouldn't know the difference between 'number 6' in the counting series and 'there are 6' in a set. This still, however, only shows that the child knows what to do in each case and that in one case the result attaches to an object and in the other that it attaches to a collection.

While in the abstract this might appear a possible origin for considerable educational difficulties, in practice this kind of misunderstanding is not something that seems to persist to plague the arithmetic teacher in the middle primary school. The reason is, I think, that the counting procedure rather neatly sets up the correct interpretation of cardinal and ordinal number. To define a cardinal number in abstract terms we say that the cardinal number of a collection of objects is three when that collection can be put in one-to-one correspondence with a 'comparison set' of three objects. If we were really to take this definition seriously we might actually walk around with a box containing three objects and get it out every time we wanted to know if a collection contained three objects. Our actual procedure it to walk around with the number names 'one', 'two', 'three' in our heads and to match these up with the new collection. Thus our actual procedure is not so very different from the ideal procedure, except that the child might not think of the words 'one', 'two' or 'three' as things. However, the presence of the written numerals 1, 2, 3 probably helps children to actually adopt something like this interpretation of the number names and so move fairly quickly to regarding 'three things' as meaning 'any collection that can be put into one-to-one correspondence with the first three number names'. In addition, as demonstrated by Piaget (1941), children between 6 and 7 realise that if collection A is in one-to-one correspondence with collection B and B with C, then A is in correspondence with C. This removes any suspicion that the comparison set has a privileged status and must give rise to the conclusion that collections with the cardinal number three are all in one-to-one correspondence with one another.

The series of number names also suggests a natural correspondence with series in time or space and children seem to develop a fairly rapid understanding of the meaning of 'first', 'second' and so on that is adequate for the needs of the middle primary years. Brainerd's (1979) training studies show that it is easy to train even preschool children to use the terms 'one', 'two', 'three' to indicate members of a series. From an educational point of view it would seem preferable to teach children to associate the names 'first', 'second', etc. with items in a series so as to emphasise the distinctive features of ordinal number. This may be difficult with very young children because of their difficulties with the 'th' sound in 'fourth', 'fifth', 'sixth', but some approximation to the adult pronunciation should be possible by about 6½ for most children.

THE NUMBER SYSTEM

The Hindu-Arabic system of representing numbers is widely used today because it is very convenient, much more so than the cumbersome Roman numerals. We use ten digits, from 0-9. The right-most digit is understood to mean the number of ones, the next digit to the left the number of tens, the next hundreds, and so on. This is only one way of representing numbers. The Roman numerals provide another and the binary numbers used by computers another. In the binary, or base two number system, the right-most digit is the ones, the next to the left the number of twos, the next the number of fours, and so on. Instead of going up by ten times as we shift along to the left we go up by two times.

It is reasonably easy to teach young children the base ten system using Dienes's base ten blocks or other materials such as Unifix. All such materials have a one, which may be a little cube or pyramid or sphere. These are then joined together to make what Dienes calls a 'long' or 'ten' which is ten of the ones strung together in a row. Ten of the longs placed side by side makes a 'flat' or 'hundred', containing a hundred ones. With Unifix materials the children can actually make up the tens and hundreds, which is probably an advantage.

Using materials of this kind young children can be encouraged to set up numbers like twenty-five or 136 as 2 tens and 5 ones, or 1 hundred, 3 tens and 6 ones. This kind of activity seems to be fairly universal in primary classrooms nowadays and provides a good way of showing children in the first two or three years of school just what it is that numbers stand for. Dienes (1960) suggests that we use a variety of different materials to do this, such as both formal apparatus and everyday objects like buttons and beans, so that children come to realise that the meaning of twenty-five is not 'two lots of ten cubes and five lots of one cube' but 'two lots of ten things and five lots of one thing'.

The most controversial issue in teaching the number system is whether to teach multibase or not. According to Dienes (1966) it helps children to understand the number system if they are taught not only numbers to the base ten but numbers in other systems like base two or five. In the Dienes base 5 multibase blocks apparatus, for instance, a long would contain 5 ones and a flat would contain 25 ones. By learning different number systems Dienes claims the child is better able to understand the base ten system.

This claim has long met with considerable scepticism. The chief reason for this is that while teaching several systems may help the child to understand that we use only one of many possible systems it is not clear that children really need to grasp this in order to understand the base ten system. It may be better to teach them the base ten system and wait until later to show them that there are other possible systems.

Practical experience has apparently sustained this kind of objection as the teaching of multibase has declined in the Anglo-Saxon world since the mid 1970s. Fehr (1966) already complained he could find no empirical study demonstrating that multibase work helps children to understand the base ten system. Lovell (1971) felt that asking children to consider a variety of number systems might involve 'formal operations' thinking and was thus inappropriate to the earlier primary years. Resnick and Ford (1981, Ch. 5) were still unable to find an adequately controlled study to demonstrate the superiority of multibase. Many practitioners now reserve multibase work in the primary years for the more able student who is better able to cope with the extra learning involved.

LEARNING ARITHMETIC

Early Counting Strategies

It used to be common for teachers to try to forbid children from doing sums on their fingers or by counting out objects. In more recent years it has been common to actually encourage children in the first years of primary school to do such problems on their fingers or by using objects like beans or cubes on the grounds that this helps them to understand the meaning of what they are doing. While this is undoubtedly true in the first stages of learning, sometimes teachers have swung to the opposite extreme and have allowed children to go on doing problems by 'counting-out' methods when they should be able to do them on paper or at least using a calculating machine. Counting out methods are slow and clumsy when applied to large numbers and so must ultimately give way to more rapid procedures. In recent years considerable interest has focused on how children progress from counting out all the objects mentioned in a problem or sum to counting out only some of them, as this represents a step on the road to performing calculations without counting out.

When presented with problems of the type $3 + 2 = ?$, young children tend to adopt one of two strategies. In the 'counting-all' strategy they go 'one, two, three, four, five'; in the 'counting-on' strategy they go 'three, four, five', thus avoiding the need to count all five numbers out.

Basic to both these procedures are an ability to keep track of the second number in order to know when to stop. Fuson (1981) and Fuson et al. (1982) have found that if this second number is four or less, then children do not need to do anything overt, like counting off fingers, to keep track.

For larger numbers, two main methods are used by young children. In the first ('counting entities'), a set of objects is produced—say, a certain number of fingers extended—and these are then counted at the same time as the number names are being said. Counting stops when the objects run out. In the second strategy, objects—again fingers are common—are produced one at a time for every counting name that goes by. Fingers are particularly useful here as most children know what five or seven fingers look like and this tells them when to stop.

These strategies are all fairly well known to teachers. Perhaps less often noticed are the various kinds of meaning that young children give to the first number to be added when they use the counting-on procedure. These can be appreciated from Fuson's (1981) study of children's addition strategies. Problems were presented to children in two forms. In one the task was simply to add together the number of shapes shown on one card to the number shown on a second card. In the other, the first number was shown only as a numeral and the second was a number of shapes.

Five of the twenty-seven children surveyed seemed to show the beginnings of an 'abbreviation' meaning for the first number. They ran through some of the counting words for the first number, but left some out, apparently being on their way to dropping out the tedious business of running through the first counting sequence, but not yet having done this.

The 'counting' meaning of the first number was illustrated by two children who pointed at the last shape on the first card when saying the number of shapes on the card and then proceeded to start on the next card. Clear indications that children understood the cardinal meaning of the first number were absent in Fuson's (1981) study. Understanding this would mean that the child knew that the last word counted for the first collection was the cardinal number of that collection. Davydov and Andronov (1981) describe some children in this kind of situation as indicating the entire first collection of objects with a sweep of the hand accompanied by the name for the number of objects (e.g. 'six') before beginning to count on for the second collection. This would seem to indicate an understanding of the cardinal meaning for the first number name used.

The fourth meaning for the first number is claimed to occur when counting out the first collection is seen as a preliminary to counting the entire collection containing both the first and second collections. Although Fuson (1981) was unable to give any convincing evidence of reactions exemplifying this fourth meaning, it does appear logically necessary for fully understanding the counting-on procedure to realise this aspect of counting-all. What must remain somewhat more doubtful at present is whether young children do fully understand the counting-all procedure. It may be that the abbreviation meaning of the first number is the one that children actually use in transition to the counting-on strategy and that they are in effect simply saving themselves time. Secanda, Fuson and Hall (1983) did

succeed in successfully training the counting-all technique using a procedure claimed to train both the abbreviation and the fourth 'inclusion'
meaning of the first number. It is still not clear from this that training on
the inclusion meaning alone would result in improvement.

In conclusion it should be pointed out that despite the considerable interest in the use of counting strategies in addition, the educational significance of such studies is still somewhat unclear. We know from formal
studies as well as from common experience that the two counting strategies ultimately give way to the more rapid methods that use a combination
of known number facts and algorithmic methods. This transition has been
extensively studied by psychologists in relation to mental arithmetic.[9]
There is no doubt that a similar transition also takes place in relation to
knowing how to do computations on paper. The educational problem, as
Fuson (1981) points out, is to know to what extent we should encourage
'counting on the fingers' as an aid to addition or other kinds of computation. As already mentioned, while this is undoubtedly helpful in the initial
stages of learning, if it persists too long it can and will discourage learning
number facts and computational methods. To give an extreme example, I
have heard teachers complain of secondary school students who need to
draw 'four lots of five' dots on a piece of paper and count them in order to
find out what 4 fives are. There is, of course, an argument that calculators
make such skills partially redundant. I shall, however, argue in more detail
later, that to compute approximations to check on our calculators we will
continue to need large parts of our existing computational skills. This
means at some point making a judgement about when counting-out procedures have served their purpose.

Word Problems

Arithmetical word problems have also been popular in recent years as a
method of encouraging children to understand what they are doing in the
first stages of arithmetic learning. A typical example would be: 'Jimmy has
three apples. He then picks four apples from a tree. How many apples does
Jimmy have?'

As with problems like $3 + 4 = ?$, the child at first generally attempts
such problems by counting out objects or fingers. To do the problem about
Jimmy and the apples the child might open out three fingers (the original
apples), then open out four more fingers (the apples picked) and then
count the fingers now opened.

It has been established by a large number of studies that variables such
as familiarity of vocabulary and syntactic complexity influence children's
ability to solve arithmetical word problems.[10] This is hardly surprising,
though it does provide a useful guide to the origins of certain kinds of
difficulties.

Much recent research has tried to look more closely at the actual processes children use to approach arithmetical problems framed in words. It is a common occurrence for teachers to find that although children can correctly solve problems like $5 - 3 = ?$ when presented as a sum in this standard format, the same children have difficulty when we say 'Farmer Brown had five cows. He sold two. How many cows did he have left?' One finding from recent research has been that when presented with such problems in a spoken form and when allowed to solve them by setting the problems up using concrete materials, even quite young children can solve them, although older children fail when they try to convert the problem to a sum on paper.[11] It seems that young children are able to succeed partly because they are not yet being encouraged to translate verbal problems into symbolic form. Representing such a problem for themselves by means of five fingers, closing up two fingers for the two cows lost and then counting the result seems to be a more natural way of solving the problem. While we know that success declines quite markedly when larger numbers are involved, it is still probably true that the expectation of writing the problem down in symbolic form is a hindrance, even for large numbers (Carpenter *et al.*, 1983).

There is thus an educational issue raised by children's early efforts to represent problems. Unfortunately a sensible resolution of this has been impeded by a major conceptual error in the way the problem has been approached in much of the most influential recent writing. Under the influence of Riley (1981) and Riley, Greeno and Heller (1983) the issue has been approached through elaborate information-processing models that make the standard information-processing assumption that children must first represent such problems in long-term memory and then use action schemes and problem-solving strategies to solve them. Unfortunately these assumptions are largely invalid in this particular instance. What actually happens is that children usually translate the instructions into a real-world set-up. An example of how this happens from Carpenter *et al.* (1983) will help to underline this point.

Carpenter *et al.* state:

> For example, to solve the following problem, most young children would make a set of objects and remove four of them. "Jan had twelve marbles. She lost four of them. How many does she have left?" On the other hand the following problem would be solved by first making a set of four objects and then incrementing the set until it contained a total of twelve objects. The answer would be found by counting the objects added to the set. "Jan has four marbles. How many more marbles does she need to have twelve marbles?"

It seems quite clear that what happens in both cases is that the successful child sets up the real-world representation and then reads the answer off this representation. The problems faced are thus those of understanding how to translate the problem into its real-world representation and which aspect of this representation represents the answer requested.

The approach to this issue suggested here indicates a resolution of a key problem. To quote Carpenter *et al.* (1983) again:

> Why are the relatively sophisticated problem-solving strategies of younger children that focus on the semantic structure of problems replaced by the superficial analysis of verbal problems found in many older children as they attempt to decide whether to add, subtract, multiply or divide?

And, it should be added, as they try to decide which numbers to subtract from or divide by which.

The answer to this is now fairly clear. The 'relatively sophisticated problem-solving strategies of younger children' are in fact non-existent. Younger children have relatively successful strategies for representing arithmetical word problems, but these strategies actually often absolve them from any need to implement a problem-solving strategy. They just read the answers off the representation. The problems that older children face also come partly from the need to devise a representation; it is the non-pictorial nature of their representations that causes difficulty. Younger children can in a sense 'see' the correspondence between the meaning of the sentences used to convey the problem and the way to proceed as they go along. Thus when the adult says 'Jan had twelve marbles', the child can put out twelve Unifix blocks or whatever. In interpreting the next piece of information the child can then refer not to traces set up in long-term memory but to the represented situation on the table: 'She lost four of them' means she lost four of these things on the table, which prompts the action of removing them. 'How many does she have left?' is now a very easy question to answer in this case as it is staring the child in the face. In the case of the questions about Jan and her marbles, the answer is more difficult to discover as the child begins by making a set of four, adds on eight so as to have twelve and must then know that it is the eight rather than the four or the twelve that is the answer.[12]

In summary, the representational strategies of young children for solving word problems are in the main what we have always taken them to be: means of avoiding the necessity for problem solving. The aim of teaching children to shift from these strategies to the use of numerals and computational methods is to give them the very powerful problem-solving techniques involved in solving equations with one unknown. The real message we should draw from work on arithmetical word problems is that it reinforces our belief that young children do not possess powerful internal problem-solving strategies for solving numerical problems. It is for this reason that we must try to help them to acquire those powerful techniques that are available once we get the problem on paper. The difficulty they face in this is to surmount the problems posed by the non-pictorial, non-graphic nature of representations that use numerals, operations and the e-quals sign.[13]

Invented Algorithms

When children are first confronted with numerical problems like $5 + 3 = ?$ they tend, as we have seen, to adopt a counting strategy. Somewhat later many children when faced with rather harder problems than this one will invent their own calculation methods, which are a compromise between the 'official' methods of the teacher and earlier counting strategies. While many of these invented methods, like the counting strategies, are rather cumbersome and take a long time, there is no harm in allowing them for a while until the child seems ready for the more powerful official proce-dures. Some of the invented strategies actually show considerably more understanding and initiative than rote application of the official methods.

A simple example of an invented algorithm is given by Ginsburg (1977). Danny was asked to add 7 and 7. He produced the right result and when asked how he did it said, 'Six and 6 are 12. Put 2 more makes 14' (Ginsburg, 1977, p. 95). One advantage of allowing children to use this kind of method for a while is that it makes them aware of the advantage of knowing one's multiplication tables.

Ginsburg's prize interviewee was Carol, 8, whom he asked to tell him the number of hours in a week. She knew there are 24 hours in a day and 7 days in a week, and when asked how many hours in a week said 'Just add them up'. She wrote down 24 seven times like this.

$$
\begin{array}{r}
24 \\
24 \\
24 \\
24 \\
24 \\
24 \\
24 \\
\hline
\end{array}
$$

To do the right-hand column she added the first 4 fours by going '4 and 4 is 8. Eight and 8 is 16.' She then counted on four for each of the next 3 fours to produce 28. She wrote the 8 units down and carried the 2 tens. This left 8 twos in the tens column and as Carol knew that 8 twos are 16 from her multiplication tables she was able to immediately write down 6 in the tens column and 1 in the hundreds. Although Carol was cumber-some in dealing with the units column she actually saved time in the tens column by noticing that the problem could be approached through multi-plication. This ability to use a known fact to provide a short cut is typical of good adult calculators, most of whom do not use the standard routines learned in school (see Reys *et al.*, 1982). For instance, most good adult calculators faced with the following addition problem will not use the standard algorithm:

$$125$$
$$25$$
$$7$$
$$50$$
$$\overline{}$$

According to the standard procedure we ought to begin with the right-hand column, add it up, carry, do the next column to the left and so on. Anyone who deals with numbers a lot will, however, instantly see that there are several multiples of 25 in this sum. I would do the problem by noticing that if we get rid of the 7 the tens and units amount to 4 twenty-fives, which, added to the 100 in the hundreds column, makes 200. The answer is therefore 207.

This procedure is typical of the short-cuts used by both Carol and good adult calculators. As far as the teacher is concerned the way to help children progress from their early invented methods is to guide them away from the use of counting methods and on to the use of methods based on number facts as these are always much quicker. It may sometimes be necessary to point out to children the time-saving value both of implementing the standard calculation procedures using remembered facts and of using remembered facts to provide short-cuts. Some children left to their own devices will cling on to counting methods in particular long after they should have transferred to more efficient strategies, probably because the counting procedures are easy to understand and they get the answer, even if laboriously. Houlihan and Ginsburg (1981) found that among 7 year olds some children used a memory strategy on addition problems with small numbers but counted for larger numbers, while others counted on the problems with small numbers but used the standard addition procedure beginning by adding up the right hand column for larger numbers. The latter procedure seems to show a healthy respect for the greater efficiency of the standard procedure when faced with large numbers. The first procedure seems likely to stem from an uncertainty about how to conceptualise larger numbers, possibly involving an inability to understand the 'hundreds, tens and units' system of place value. In such cases attention to the concept of place value as well as careful explanation of the greater speed of the standard procedure would seem to be indicated. One might even think of a competition between two groups of children, one using counting and the other using the standard calculation procedure, in order to drive this point home.

Understanding Algorithms

When we teach methods for performing arithmetical computations to young children we have a choice as to how to proceed. In asking children to perform $18 + 31$ we may either just tell them what to do without any explanation, or we can give an explanation like the following rationale: '$18 + 31$ is the same as 1 ten plus 8 ones plus 3 tens plus 1 one. We can group together the ones and the tens so we get 1 ten plus 3 tens and 8 ones plus 1 one. We can write this as 4 tens and 9 ones.' This last step is the hardest as it involves the distributive law of addition over multiplication that says for any numbers A, B, C it is true that $A \times C + B \times C = (A + B) \times C$. This is something that young children find hard to grasp even on an intuitive level.

For the classroom teacher the questions of by what means and to what extent to teach understanding of the computational methods involved in doing sums or in solving word problems are of great importance. Unfortunately, however, both classroom teachers and researchers have often been confused about what they mean by 'teaching for understanding' in this area.[14]

As Gagné (1983) has pointed out, there are two ways of teaching understanding of the computational algorithms. The first is 'concrete' and involves encouraging the kind of counting methods we have encountered in previous sections. As Gagné notes, this kind of activity is fine for developing an understanding of how to get from real situations or from word problems to symbolic presentations of such problems, such as $2 \times 3 = ?$. However, it is not fine as a method of actually carrying out computations for 12 or 14 year olds. There is little doubt that the excessive reliance on counting methods by older children is at least partly responsible for some of the dire statistics on the decline of numeracy in the United States cited by Gagné.

The other kind of understanding is what Gagné calls the 'abstract' approach. This is when we explain to children that the reason we write the tens under the tens and the ones under the ones is so we can add like to like. It is also involved when we explain that in 'carrying' the tens that have accumulated in the ones column we are also making sure that like stays with like. Gagné (1983) claims, without citing any research, that this kind of explanation is also detrimental to the efficient learning of computational skills. In point of fact, however, there is a body of research that shows that at least for the child who is average or above average in mathematical ability it is advantageous to teach at least part of the rationale for computations. I must, however, stress at the outset that this should not be taken to mean that the less able can necessarily benefit from this, nor that the more able benefit from an insistence that they understand every aspect of the rationale for computations. The reason for stressing these points is firstly that much of the research on this issue cites improvements in group means as a result of teaching for understanding. In those few studies that have looked at ability levels we find, as classroom experience would suggest, that the less able may actually do better with rote learning methods. Secondly, the teaching methods that have been used in such studies have often looked at the effects of teaching only limited aspects of understanding the rationale for computational methods. Certain aspects of such a rationale may stretch the understanding of all but the most able students until the upper primary years.

Brownell and Moser (1949) in an influential study compared the teaching of 'borrowing' in subtraction by meaningful and rote methods. Here meaning took the form of abstract rationale rather than concrete counting. The most successful meaningful method was that of meaningful decomposition. Consider the following subtraction sum:

$$\begin{array}{r} 46 \\ 39 \\ \hline \end{array}$$

Here it would be explained to the child that we can't take 9 from 6 so we decompose the 4 tens on the top into 3 tens on the left and 1 on the right, which is used to make the ones into 16.

In Brownell and Moser's study it was found that this method given with rationale was superior to a method involving rote learning of the procedure. Despite the widespread influence of this study it contains a basic design flaw. The rote learning conditions were not encouraged to write down the borrowed and paid back tens but to perform the procedure mentally. However, young children tend to forget to pay back and this put the rote learners at a quite unfair disadvantage.

There is another and perhaps more central aspect of the rationale for computations that seems to have received little attention in controlled studies until recently: understanding the place value system that assigns ones to the right-hand column, tens to the next on the left and so on. One reason for this may have been that during the 1960s, under the influence of Dienes, attention was focused on the kind of super-sophisticated understanding of the place value system encouraged by encounters with multibase. Both Fehr (1966) and Resnick and Ford (1981) were unable to find any study substantiating an improvement in understanding the base ten system as a result of such instruction, let alone a transfer to arithmetic learning. Recently, however, Greaves (1983) has reported a study showing that simple instruction in the base ten system encouraging the transition from groups of objects and pictures to their representation in the base 10 system did result in quite considerable improvement in arithmetical performance. Presumably the children who had special instruction in the place value system were better able to assimilate concurrent instruction in computational methods as well as perhaps being able to transfer their understanding during practice exercises.[15]

There have been comparatively few well-designed attempts to look at interactions between teaching methods and ability in arithmetic learning.[16] A particular difficulty of research in this area is illustrated by Brownell and Moser's (1949) finding that while explanation of the borrowing procedures for subtraction was generally superior there were some schools where previously instruction had been entirely by rote and children appeared unable to profit from explanations. It seems they were so unused to explanation they rejected it. Students' reactions to explanations are likely to be influenced by their previous experiences.

I have recently completed a study in which it was found that an individualised arithmetic programme involving extensive exercises aimed at developing a full rationale for computational methods was greatly superior to traditional instruction concentrating on the meaning of the operations and rote learning of computational procedures for children above average in arithmetical achievement. For below average ability children the traditional method was marginally but not significantly superior. This study would seem to show that abstract rationale is more suitable for the higher range of ability (Langford, 1986b). This applies to students who had probably, like most children in the early grades, had considerable concrete explanation but little abstract rationale.

In conclusion, there are two kinds of meaningful instruction in arithmetic, the concrete use of counting and the giving of an abstract rationale. There is little doubt that excessive reliance on counting methods in the later primary grades is detrimental to the achievement of computational facility, though in the earlier grades counting probably helps children to understand the transition from real world situations to symbols. It is probably worth presenting all children with the abstract rationale for computations but those who have difficulty with arithmetic often experience problems in grasping such a rationale in its entirety. For such children it may be more important to allow simple rote learning of a procedure to obtain a correct answer than to insist on full understanding. While many programmes discourage a competitive attitude among children most children will eventually meet an expectation from a parent or a secondary school teacher that they successfully perform such computations. So long as a child knows when to apply the right operation it is not of great significance if they fail to understand the rationale for the computational method. Some writers, such as Gagné (1983), point out that when the skilled mathematician actually implements procedures like differentiation or even the humble arithmetical algorithms they do not simultaneously recall their rationale. It should also be borne in mind that young children are very much influenced by previous expectations about the depth of understanding required. We must often be prepared to be sobered by that awful rejoinder of children who learn by rote and reject alternative methods: 'We don't do them like that!'

Debugging Procedures

Another issue that has been popular in recent years is how to debug errors in students' algorithmic procedures. The following example from Brown and Burton (1978) shows the kind of problem involved. A student was generally proficient at adding up two and three digit numbers, except for the following examples:

$$
\begin{array}{r} 87 \\ +93 \\ \hline 11 \end{array}
\qquad
\begin{array}{r} 679 \\ +794 \\ \hline 111 \end{array}
\qquad
\begin{array}{r} 923 \\ +481 \\ \hline 114 \end{array}
$$

The explanation was that every time the student had to carry, he wrote down the digit to be carried as part of the answer and just ignored the digit that should have gone in the answer. Brown and Burton (1978) describe an elaborate computer simulation model called BUGGY that successfully models most common errors in arithmetical procedures.

BUGGY is designed to diagnose errors using only information from the student's written sums. Fortunately, teachers are in a better position as they can actually ask students why they did what they did. At the most general level teachers should thus be aware that many errors that appear random (if not downright crazy) are a result of consistently using wrong procedures and should try to ask students about why they do what they do. Brown and Burton (1978) also found that exposing trainee teachers to BUGGY considerably improved their ability to detect bugs. Unfortunately this is not easily available. Ashlock (1982) does, however, provide a slightly less rigorous but nonetheless valuable introduction to common types of computational error.[17]

Approximation Techniques

It is sometimes thought that with the widespread use of calculators the need for children to learn the laborious traditional techniques of computation will gradually disappear. All that will be needed, so the argument goes, will be for children to learn approximation techniques to check up on the results of their calculations.

The flaw in this argument appears in the words 'all that will be needed'. In reality computational approximation tends to require a high degree of facility in mental arithmetic and a wide command of number facts and short cuts. It is more like something that children need in addition to a command of traditional computational skills than something they can acquire instead of them. Having said this, it remains true that long multi-plication and long division in particular may eventually become redundant skills as few people can apply these procedures mentally and thus they are of little value for deriving approximations.

To appreciate more clearly what is involved in approximating a calcula-tion we may consider some examples from Reys *et al.* (1982). As a result of interviews with secondary school students and adults these authors found three main kinds of strategy used in estimation by those of good mathematical ability. In 'reformulation' the usual tactic is to round the numbers up or down so as to obtain round figures that can be more easily calculated. Consider for instance:

$$8,127 \overline{) \; 474,257}$$

One interviewee said, 'I just rounded it (the dividend) up to 480,000 and knocked that (the divisor) down to 8,000. It has to be about 60.' Notice that to reason like this the student must have a good grasp of place value, must understand the technique of dividing dividend and divisor by a common factor (in this case this involves 'knocking off' the three noughts) and must know that 6×8 is 48 in order to mentally divide 48 by 8.

In 'translation' the structure of the problem is altered either so that operations are performed in a changed order or so that the actual opera-tions are altered. Strictly speaking, these are short-cut computational methods that are used once the figures in the problem have been converted to round numbers. As an example of altering the order of operations:

$$\frac{347 \times 6}{43}$$

The interviewee said 'It would be easiest to divide the 6 and 43 first, which is about 7, so 347/7 is about 50.' Here there is no law that compels us to do the top line first but we know the line underneath it is supposed to be 'like a bracket' so we are tempted to work inside the bracket first. Ex-perienced calculators, however, will most often begin by trying to 'cancel out' common factors in the top and bottom line and they know that when the top and bottom lines are linked only by multiplication signs we can cancel out common factors from any pair of numbers, provided one is on the top and the other on the bottom. Notice that apart from the use of rounding up and down here the approximation skill is entirely one of con-ventional mental computation.

An example of altering the operation involved is when we have a whole list of approximately similar numbers to add and having rounded them all up or down to the same number we then multiply by the number of num-bers in the list to get the answer. Notice that having used rounding this is again simply a conventional computational method and is in fact very similar to one that Carol used to add up the 8 twos in her tens column.

In compensation some effort is made to compensate for error that might arise as a result of rounding up or down. Thus in addition or multiplication we try to compensate for rounding up some figures by rounding down others; in subtraction or division we need to compensate for addition on one side of the operation by addition on the other and we need to compensate for subtraction by subtraction. Another tactic is to add or subtract something at the end of the calculation to make up for errors produced by rounding.

Reys *et al.* (1982) looked at the characteristics of good estimators and found them to have, as we might expect, 'a quick and accurate recall of basic facts for all operations', an understanding of place value and 'quick and efficient use of mental computation'. 'All estimators exhibited well-developed skill with multiples of 10 or a limited number of digits, and many others were fluent in mentally computing with larger numbers, more digits and even different types of numbers (e.g. fractions).' Good approximators also understood basic arithmetical laws, including the distributive, associative and commutative laws and knew how to apply them to choice of order of operations. In addition to these characteristics, which might be summarised as a good knowledge of basic concepts and mental arithmetic procedures, good approximators were also adept in applying the strategies of rounding and compensation, which are peculiar to approximation techniques.[18]

There have been a number of studies showing that the teaching of rounding techniques can improve the ability of 9, 10 and 11 year olds to make good approximations.[19] Schoen *et al.* (1981) also found the 'front-end' technique to be effective. This is a kind of 'rough rounding' in which the round figure is derived from the 'front-end' figure. Thus 573×4 becomes 500×4. In the more advanced use of rounding, 573 would become 600×4 as 573 is much nearer 600 than 500. As we might expect, Schoen *et al.* (1981) found progress towards good approximation was generally associated with a shift away from front-end towards more exact rounding. With younger children the front-end technique may, however, provide a simplified beginning.

While Nelson (1967) found that the learning of estimation techniques seemed to interfere with exact computational skills, Schoen *et al.* (1981) found no such interference. Nelson attributed his unexpected finding to the fact that students taught to estimate took longer and thus finished fewer items on his computation test rather than to any decline in accuracy. There is no reason to expect such a decline in accuracy except if students confuse estimation with precise computation. It is probably worth emphasising the difference.

CONCLUSIONS

This is an area in which the shift away from Piagetian beliefs has quite considerable implications for practice. Such implications for the teaching of geometry and set theory have been outlined at the beginning of the chapter. In the teaching of arithmetic the questioning of three Piagetian beliefs in particular has considerable practical significance. The Piagetian belief that children need to approach arithmetic through aspects of set theory has been doubted both because there is no logical dependence of arithmetic upon set theory and because many concepts in set theory seem to develop later than the corresponding concepts in arithmetic. The Piagetian belief that children cannot understand counting until they understand conservation of correspondence has also been doubted. The weight of current opinion is in favour of the reverse dependence: children probably learn a lot about conservation of correspondence from counting. Piaget believed that for children to understand addition and subtraction they needed a simultaneous appreciation of the parts and whole of a collection. Whether one regards this as true or not depends partly upon one's definition of understanding. A really complete understanding of addition and subtraction would require this. Much of the recent literature on early counting strategies and on word problems assumes that this is also necessary for successful solution of simple problems using counting-out strategies. I have argued that this is not so and that the chief difficulty young children face in dealing with word problems is in translating the real-world situation into a concrete set-up. It was also argued that the development of good arithmetical approximation techniques depends upon developing mental arithmetic techniques using exact computational methods. For this reason it is unlikely that widespread use of calculators will do more than reduce emphasis upon long multiplication and division.

FURTHER READING

On conservation learning see either Acredolo (1981) or Acredolo (1982); on number concepts Brainerd (1979) and Gelman and Gallistel (1978) are both worth looking at (given in each case the cautions expressed in the text). Of more recent studies Michie (1985) is perhaps the most interesting. On the number system see Resnick and Ford (1981, Ch. 5); on early counting strategies see Fuson (1981) and Fuson *et al.* (1982); for two views of word problems see on the one hand Riley *et al.* (1983) and Kintsch and Greeno (1985) and on the other Langford (1986a), or the less readily available Briars and Larkin (1984); on invented algorithms see Ginsburg (1977); on understanding algorithms see Resnick and Ford (1981) and Gagné (1983); on debugging procedures and typical errors see especially Ashlock (1982) and also Brown and Burton (1978), Cox (1975), Brannin (1983); on approximation techniques see Reys *et al.* (1982) and Rubenstein (1985).

NOTES

1. See also Sommerville and Bryant (1985).
2. See for instance Brainerd (1975), Langford (1981).
3. Wallach (1969), Langford (1979, Ch. 10).
4. This doubt is reinforced by the findings of Moore *et al.* (1984) and Halford and Boyle (1984).
5. See Bryant (1974), Brainerd (1979).
6. Nelson and Bartley (1961), Klahr and Wallace (1976).
7. Potter and Levy (1968), Gelman and Gallistel (1978, Ch. 7).
8. For the Piagetian view see Lovell (1971, Ch. 2), Copeland (1974).
9. Groen and Poll (1973), Parkman (1972), Ashcraft and Battaglia (1978), Ashcraft (1982), Brainerd (1983).
10. For reviews see Hollander (1978), Jerman (1973-74), Jerman and Rees (1972).
11. Carpenter and Moser (1982), Carpenter *et al.* (1983).
12. Some of Riley, Greeno and Heller's (1983) problem types do require internal representation as the child tries to set up the real-world representation. The difference between these and the simpler problem types can be used to predict problem difficulty. See Langford (1986a).
13. The influence of teaching the part-whole relationship upon arithmetical word problems has been studied by Wolters (1983).
14. Considerable ambiguity of this kind can for instance be found in the classic studies of Brownell and Chazal (1935) and McConnell (1934).
15. Davis and McKnight (1980) found, however, that in one type of problem children who understood the place value system failed to apply this knowledge to algorithmic procedures. It would be interesting to know more about the generality of this and its reasons.
16. Anderson (1949) claimed rote learning favoured the high achiever, but Cronbach and Snow (1977) showed deficiencies in the statistical analysis. Studies by Thiele (1938) and McConnell (1934) involved Gagné's (1983) 'concrete' rationale and reached opposing conclusions, possibly because answers achieved by counting were not separated from those achieved by automatic response.
17. See Cox (1975), Brown and Burton (1978), Brannin (1983).
18. The positive association between rapid computational ability and ability in approximations has also been verified by Paul (1981) and Rubenstein (1985).
19. Nelson (1967), Sutherlin (1977), Hall (1966), Schoen *et al.* (1981).

BIBLIOGRAPHY

Chapter 1

Abraham, M. R. and Renner, J. W. (1986) 'The sequence of learning cycle activities in high school chemistry', *Journal of Research in Science Teaching*, 23, 121-43

Anderson, J. H. and Armbruster, B. B. (1984) 'Studying', in P. D. Pearson (ed.), *Handbook of Reading Research*, Longman, New York

Ault, R. (1977) *Children's Cognitive Development*, Oxford University Press, New York

Ausubel, D., Novak, J. D. and Hanesian, H. (1978) *Educational Psychology, A Cognitive View*, 2nd edn, Holt, Rinehart and Winston, New York

Bennett, N. (1977) *Teaching Style and Pupil Progress*, Open Books, London

Brainerd, C. J. (1983) 'Young children's mental arithmetic errors: a working memory analysis', *Child Development*, 54, 812-30

————— and Kingma, J. (1985) 'On the independence of short term memory and working memory in cognitive development', *Cognitive Psychology*, 17, 210-47

Bullock, M. *et al.* (1982) 'The development of causal reasoning', in W. J. Friedman (ed.), *The Developmental Psychology of Time*, Academic Press, New York

————— (1985) 'Causal reasoning and developmental change over the preschool years', *Human Development*, 28, 169-91

Case, R. (1979) 'The underlying mechanism of intellectual development', in J. Biggs and J. Kirby (eds), *Instructional Processes and Individual Differences in Learning*, Academic Press, New York

Dunn, C. S. (1983) 'The influence of instructional methods on concept learning', *Science Education*, 67, 647-56

Ennis, R. H. (1976) 'An alternative to Piaget's conceptualisation of logical competence', *Child Development*, 47, 903-19

Fischer, K. W. (1980) 'A theory of cognitive development: the control and construction of hierarchies of skills', *Psychological Review*, 87, 477-531

————— and Pipp, S. L. (1984) 'Processes of cognitive development: optimal level and skill acquisition', in R. J. Sternberg (ed.), *Mechanisms of Cognitive Development*, Freeman, New York

Gagné, R. M. (1984) *The Conditions of Learning*, 4th edn, Holt Saunders, New York

Halford, G. S. and Wilson, W. H. (1980) 'A category theory approach to cognitive development', *Cognitive Psychology*, 12, 356-411

Inhelder, B. and Piaget, J. (1955) *The Growth of Logical Thinking From Childhood to Adolescence*, Basic Books, New York

Karplus, R. (1980) 'Teaching for the development of reasoning', in A. E. Lawson (ed.), *1980 AETS Yearbook*, Eric, Columbus

Kennedy, K. J. (1983) 'Assessing the relationship between information processing capacity and historical understanding', *Theory and Research in Social Education*, 11, 1-22

Langford, P. E. (1974) 'The development of concepts of infinity and limit in mathematics', *Archives de Psychologie*, 42, 311-22

———— (1980) 'Review of J. A. Keats, K. Collis and G. Halford (eds) *Cognitive Development*, 1978, Wiley, New York,' *Australian Journal of Psychology*, 32, 69-71

———— (1981) 'A longitudinal study of children's understanding of logical laws in arithmetic and Boolean algebra', *Educational Psychology*, 1, 119-39

———— (1984) 'A critique of Halford and Wilson's approach to cognitive development', *Research in Mathematics Education in Australia*, 1 (2), 34-40

Lott, G. W. (1983) 'The effect of inquiry teaching and advance organisers upon student outcomes in science education', *Journal of Research in Science Teaching*, 20, 437-51

McKinney, C. W. *et al.* (1983) 'The effectiveness of three methods of teaching social studies concepts to fourth-grade students', *American Education Research Journal*, 20, 663-70

Norman, D. A. (1980) 'What goes on in the mind of the learner', in W. J. McKeachie (ed.), *Learning, Cognition and College Teaching*, Jossey-Bass, San Francisco

Osherson, D. N. (1974) *Logical Abilities in Children* (Vol. 1), Wiley, New York

Pascual-Leone, J. (1971) 'A mathematical model for the transition rule in Piaget's stages', *Acta Psychologica*, 32, 301-45

Piaget, J. and Inhelder, B. (1969) *The Psychology of the Child*, Routledge, London

Seltman, M. and Seltman, P. (1985) *Piaget's Logic*, Allen and Unwin, London

Siegler, R. S. (1981) 'Developmental sequences within and between concepts', *Monographs of the Society for Research in Child Development*, 46 (2)

Spiker, C. C. and Cantor, J. H. (1983) 'Components in the hypothesis-testing strategies of young children', in T. J. Tighe and B. E. Shepp (eds), *Perception, Cognition and Development*, Erlbaum, Hillsdale

Sternberg, R. J. (1979) 'Developmental patterns in the encoding and combination of logical connectives', *Journal of Experimental Child Psychology*, 28, 469-98

Tennyson, R. D. *et al.* (1981) 'Concept learning effectiveness using prototype and skill development presentation forms', *Journal of Educational Psychology*, 74, 329-44

Trabasso, T. (1978) 'On the estimation of parameters and the evaluation of mathematical models: a reply to Pascual-Leone', *Journal of Experimental Child Psychology*, 26, 41-5

————— and Foellinger, D. B. (1978) 'Information-processing capacity in children: a test of Pascual-Leone's model', *Journal of Experimental Child Psychology*, 26, 1-17

Whiteley, J. (1985) 'Control of children's observing responses during information feedback during discrimination learning', *Journal of Experimental Child Psychology*, 39, 245-69

Wilson, K. W. (1980) *From Associations to Structure*, North Holland, Amsterdam

Chapter 2

Adams, M. J. and Huggins, A. W. F. (1985) 'The growth of children's sight vocabulary', *Reading Research Quarterly*, 20, 262-81

Agnew, A. T. (1982) 'Using children's dictated stories to assess code consciousness', *Reading Teacher*, 35, 450-54

Applebee, A. N. (1978) *The Child's Conception of Story*, University of Chicago Press, Chicago

Bartlett, F. C. (1932) *Remembering*, Cambridge University Press, Cambridge

Beech, J. R. (1985) *Learning to Read*, Croom Helm, London

Bellefroid, B. de and Ferreiro, E. (1979) 'La segmentation de mots chez l'enfant', *Archives de Psychologie*, 47, 1-36

Berthoud, I. (1978) 'An experimental study of children's ideas about language', in A. Sinclair *et al.* (eds), *The Child's Conception of Language*, Verlag, New York

————— (1980) *La Reflexion Metalinguistique chez l'Enfant*, Université de Genève, Ph.D. thesis

Black, J. B. and Wilensky, R. (1979) 'An evaluation of story grammars', *Cognitive Science*, 3, 213-30

————— and Bower, G. H. (1980) 'Story understanding as problem solving', *Poetics*, 9, 223-50

Bohannon, J. (1975) 'The relationship between syntax discrimination and sentence imitation in children', *Child Development*, 46, 444-51

Botvin, G. J. and Sutton-Smith, B. (1977) 'Narrative structures in children's spontaneous stories', *Developmental Psychology*, 13, 377-88

Boutet, J., Gauthier, F. and Saint-Pierre, M. (1983) 'Savoir dire sur la phrase', *Archives de Psychologie*, 51, 205-228

Bransford, J. D., Barclay, J. R. and Franks, J. J. (1972) 'Sentence memory: a constructive versus interpretive approach', *Cognitive Psychology*, 3, 192-209

———— and Johnson, M. K. (1972) 'Contextual prerequisites for understanding: some investigations of comprehension and recall', *Journal of Verbal Learning*, 11, 717-26

Briggs, P. *et al.* (1985) 'The effects of sentence context on good and poor readers', *Reading Research Quarterly*, 20, 54-61

Brown, A. L. (1975) 'Recognition, reconstruction and recall of narrative sequences', *Child Development*, 46, 156-66

———— (1978) 'Knowing when, where and how to remember: a problem of metacognition', in R. Glaser (ed.), *Advances in Instructional Psychology*, Erlbaum, Hillsdale

———— (1980) 'Metacognitive development and reading', in R. Spiro *et al.* (eds), *Theoretical Issues in Reading Comprehension*, Erlbaum, Hillsdale

———— and Day, J. D. (1983) 'Macrorules for summarizing texts: the development of expertise', *Journal of Verbal Learning and Verbal Behaviour*, 22, 1-14

———— and Smiley, S. S. (1977) 'Rating and importance of structural units of prose passages: a problem of metacognitive development', *Child Development*, 48, 1-8

———— and ———— (1978) 'The development of strategies for summarising texts', *Child Development*, 49, 1076-88

————, ———— and Lawton, S. C. (1978) 'The effects of experience on the selection of suitable retrieval cues for studying texts', *Child Development*, 49, 829-35

Bryant, P. and Bradley, L. (1985) *Children's Reading Problems*, Blackwell, Oxford

Canney, G. and Winograd, P. (1979) 'Schemata for reading and comprehension performance', Tech. Report, No. 120, Center for the Study of Reading, University of Illinois, Urbana

Chall, J. S. (1979) 'The great debate: ten years later, with a modest proposal for reading stages', in L. B. Resnick and P. A. Weaver (eds), *Theory and Practice of Early Reading*, Vol. 1, Erlbaum, Hillsdale

Chomsky, N. (1965) *Aspects of the Theory of Syntax*, MIT Press, Cambridge, Massachusetts

Clark, E. (1978) 'Awareness of language: some evidence from what children say and do', in A. Sinclair *et al.* (eds), *The Child's Conception of Language*, Springer-Verlag, New York

Clay, M. M. (1972a) *Concepts About Print Test*, Heinemann, Auckland
———— (1972b) *The Early Detection of Reading Difficulties*, Heinemann, Auckland
———— (1972c) *Reading: The Patterning of Complex Behaviour*, Heinemann, Auckland
Cook, L.K. and Mayer, R. E. (1983) 'Reading strategies training for meaningful learning from prose', in M. Pressley and J. R. Levin (eds), *Cognitive Strategy Research*, Springer-Verlag, New York
Dasen, P. R. (1975) 'Concrete operational development in three cultures', *Journal of Cross-Cultural Psychology*, 6, 156-72
———— (1977) 'Are cognitive processes universal?', in N. Warren (ed.), *Studies in Cross-Cultural Psychology*, Vol. 1, Academic Press, London
———— (1980) 'Psychological differentiation and operational development: a cross-cultural link', *Quarterly Newsletter of Lab. of Comp. Human Cognition*, 2, 81-86
Day, H. D. and Day, K. C. (1979a) 'Item and factor analysis of the concepts about print test', unpublished paper, Department of Psychology and Philosophy, Texas Women's University, Texas
———— and ———— (1979b) 'Test-retest and split-half reliability of concepts about print test and record of oral language', unpublished paper, Department of Psychology and Philosophy, Texas Women's University, Texas
Denhiere, G. and Le Ny J.-F. (1980) 'Relative importance of meaningful units in comprehension and recall of narratives by children and adults', *Poetics*, 9, 147-61
Donaldson, M. (1978) *Children's Minds*, Fontana, London
Dooling, D. J. and Lachman, R. (1972) 'Effects of comprehension on retention of prose', *Journal of Experimental Psychology*, 88, 216-22
Downing, J. (1970) 'Children's concepts of language in learning to read', *Educational Research*, 12, 106-12
———— (1979) *Reading and Reasoning*, Springer-Verlag, New York
Edwards, A. D. (1976) *Language in Culture and Class*, Heinemann, London
Ehri, L. C. (1975) 'Word consciousness in readers and prereaders', *Journal of Educational Psychology*, 67, 204-12
———— (1979) 'Linguistic insight: threshold of reading acquisition', in T. G. Walker and G. E. Mackinnon (eds), *Reading Research: Advances in Theory and Practice*, Academic Press, New York
Fayol, M. (1978) 'Les conservations narratives chez l'enfant', *Enfance*, 4, 247-59
Fraisse, P. (1963) *The Psychology of Time*, Harper and Row, New York
Francis, H. (1974) 'Social background, speech and learning to read', *British Journal of Educational Psychology*, 44, 290-9
———— (1982) *Learning to Read*, Allen and Unwin, London

Freebody, P. and Tirre, W. C. (1985) 'Achievement outcomes of two reading programmes', *British Journal of Educational Psychology*, 55, 53-60

Gleitman, L., Gleitman, H. and Shipley, E. (1972) 'The emergence of child as grammarian', *Cognition*, 1, 136-64

Glenn, C. G. (1980) 'Relationship between story content and structure', *Journal of Educational Psychology*, 72, 550-66

Glucksberg, S., Krauss, R. M. and Higgins, E. (1975) 'The development of referential communication skills', in F. D. Horowitz (ed.), *Review of Child Development Research*, University of Chicago Press, Chicago

Goetz, E. T. and Ambruster, B. B. (1980) 'Psychological correlates of text structure', in R. J. Spiro *et al.* (eds), *Theoretical Issues in Reading Comprehension*, Erlbaum, Hillsdale

Goodman, K. S. (1967) 'Reading: a psycholinguistic guessing game', *Journal of the Reading Specialist*, 5, 126-135

————— (1968) *The Psycholinguistic Nature of the Reading Process*, Wayne State University Press, Detroit

————— (1970) 'Psycholinguistic universals in the reading process', *Journal of Typographic Research*, 4, 103-10

Hakes, D. (1980) *The Emergence of Metalinguistic Abilities in Children*, Springer-Verlag, New York

Harding, L. M. *et al.* (1985) 'The changing pattern of reading errors and reading style from 5 to 11 years of age', *British Journal of Educational Psychology*, 55, 45-52

Hiebert, E. H. (1980) 'The relationship of logical reasoning ability, oral language comprehension, and home experiences to preschool children's print awareness', *Journal of Reading Behaviour*, 12, 313-24

————— (1981) 'Developmental patterns and inter-relationships of preschool children's print awareness', *Reading Research Quarterly*, 16, 236-60

Holden M. and McGintie, W. (1972) 'Children's conceptions of word boundaries in speech and print', *Journal of Educational Psychology*, 63, 551-7

Hoppe-Graff, S., Scholer, H. and Schell, M. (1980) *Zur analyse der erzahlungen von kindern im pra und konkreptoperationalen entwicklungsstadium*, Lehrstul Psychologie III, University of Mannheim, Mannheim

————— and ————— (1980) *Wie gut verstehen und behalten kinder einfache geschichten?*, Lehrstuhl Psychologie III, University of Mannheim, Mannheim

Hudson, J. and Nelson, K. (1983) 'Effects of script structure on children's story recall', *Developmental Psychology*, 19, 625-35

Huttenlocher, J. (1964) 'Children's language: word-phrase relationship', *Science*, 143, 264-5

James, S. and Miller, J. (1973) 'Children's awareness of semantic constraints in sentences', *Child Development*, 44, 69-76

Johns, J. L. (1980) 'First graders' concepts about print', *Reading Research Quarterly*, 15, 529-549

Johnson, N. S. and Mandler, J. M. (1980) 'A tale of two structures: underlying and surface forms of stories', *Poetics*, 9, 51-86

Johnson-Laird, P. N. *et al.* (1984) 'Only connections: a critique of semantic networks', *Psychological Bulletin*, 96, 292-315

Kennedy, A. (1984) *The Psychology of Reading*, Methuen, London

Kintsch, W. (1977) 'On comprehending stories', in M. A. Just and P. Carpenter (eds), *Cognitive Processes in Comprehension*, Erlbaum, Hillsdale

———— and Greene, E. (1978) 'The role of culture specific schemata in the comprehension and recall of stories', *Discourse Processes*, 1, 1-13

———— and Van Dijk, T. A. (1978) 'Toward a model of text comprehension and production', *Psychological Review*, 85, 363-94

Koblinski, S. A. and Cruse, D. F. (1981) 'The role of frameworks in children's retention of sex-related story content', *Journal of Experimental Child Psychology*, 31, 321-31

Lakoff, G. (1971) 'On generative semantics', in D. D. Steinberg and J. A. Jakobovits (eds), *Semantics*, Cambridge University Press, Cambridge

Lesgold, A. M. and Perfetti, C. A. (1978) 'Interactive processes in reading comprehension', *Discourse Processes*, 1, 323-36

Liberman, I. (1973) 'Segmentation of the spoken word and reading acquisition', *Bulletin of the Orton Society*, 23, 65-77

Liberman, J., Shankweiler, D., Fischer, F. and Carter, B. (1974) 'Explicit syllable and phoneme segmentation in the young child', *Journal of Experimental Child Psychology*, 18, 201-12

McCartney, D. A. and Nelson, K. (1981) 'Children's use of scripts in story recall', *Discourse Processes*, 4, 59-70

McConaughy, M. (1985) 'Good and poor readers' comprehension of story structure', *Reading Research Quarterly*, 20, 219-32

Mandler, J. M. and Johnson, N. S. (1977) 'Remembrance of things passed: story structure and recall', *Cognitive Psychology*, 9, 111-151

Maratsos, M. P. (1973) 'Nonegocentric communication abilities in preschool children', *Child Development*, 44, 697-700

Markman, E. M. (1977) 'Realizing that you don't understand: a preliminary investigation', *Child Development*, 48, 936-92

———— (1979) 'Realizing that you don't understand: elementary schoolchildren's awareness of inconsistencies', *Child Development*, 50, 643-55

———— (1981) 'Comprehension monitoring', in W. P. Dickson (ed.), *Children's Oral Communication Skills*, Academic Press, New York

Mattingly, I. G. (1972) 'Reading, the linguistic process and linguistic awareness', in J. F. Kavanagh and I. G. Mattingly (eds), *Language By Ear and Eye*, MIT Press, Cambridge, Massachusetts
———— (1978) 'The psycholinguistic basis of linguistic awareness', paper presented at the annual meeting of the National Reading Conference, St Petersburg
———— (1979) 'Reading, linguistic awareness and language acquisition', paper presented at the International Reading Association meeting, University of Victoria, British Columbia
Mayfield, M. I. (1983) 'Code systems instruction and kindergarten children's perceptions of the nature and purpose of reading', *Journal of Educational Research*, 76, 161-8
Menig-Peterson, C. L. (1975) 'The modification of communicative behaviour in pre-school aged children as a function of listener's perspective', *Child Development*, 46, 1015-18
Morris, D. (1980) *Beginning Readers' Concept of Word and its Relationship to Phoneme Segmentation Ability*, University of Virginia, Virginia, Ph.D. thesis
Morrison, F. J. (1984) 'Reading disability: a problem in rule learning and word decoding', *Development Review*, 4, 36-47
Nezworski, T., Stein, N. L. and Trabasso, T. (1982) 'Story structure versus content in children's recall', *Journal of Verbal Learning and Verbal Behaviour*, 21, 196-206
Oakhill, J. (1984) 'Inferential and memory skills in children's comprehension of stories', *British Journal of Educational Psychology*, 54, 31-9
Osherson, D. and Markman, E. (1975) 'Language and the ability to evaluate contradictions and tautologies', *Cognition*, 3, 213-26
Paris, S. G. and Lindauer, B. K. (1976) 'The role of inference in children's comprehension and memory for sentences', *Cognitive Psychology*, 8, 217-227
———— and ———— (1982) 'The development of cognitive skills during childhood', in B. Wollman (ed.), *Handbook of Developmental Psychology*, Prentice-Hall, New York
———— and Upton, L. R. (1976) 'Children's memory for inferential relationships in prose', *Child Development*, 45, 659-68
Paterson, C. J. and Kister, M. C. (1981) 'The development of listener skills for referential communication', in W. P. Dickson (ed.), *Children's Oral Communication Skills*, Academic Press, New York
Pearson, P. D., Hensen, J. and Gordon, J. (1979) 'The effect of background information on young children's comprehension of explicit and implicit information', *Journal of Reading Behavior*, 11, 201-9
Perfetti, C. A. and Lesgold, A. M. (1978) 'Discourse, comprehension and individual differences', in P. Carpenter and M. Just (eds), *Cognitive Processes in Comprehension*, Erlbaum, Hillsdale

————— and ————— (1979) 'Coding and comprehension in skilled reading', in L. B. Resnick and P. A. Weaver (eds), *Theory and Practice of Early Reading*, Vol. 1, Erlbaum, Hillsdale

Piaget, J. (1969) *The Child's Conception of Time*, Routledge and Kegan Paul, London

Prawat, R. S., Cancelli, A. and Cook, B. (1976) 'A developmental study of constructive memory', *Journal of Psychology*, 92, 257-60

Propp, V. (1968) *The Morphology of the Folktale*, University of Texas Press, Austin

Read, C. (1973) 'Children's awareness of language, with emphasis on sound systems', in A. Sinclair *et al.*, (eds), *The Child's Conception of Language*, Springer-Verlag, New York

Reid, D. K. and Hresko, W. P. (1980) 'A developmental study of the relation between oral language and early reading in learning disabled and normally achieving children', *Learning Disability Quarterly*, 3, 54-61

Reid, J. F. (1958) 'A study of thirteen beginners in reading', *Acta Psychologica*, 14, 294-313

————— (1966) 'Learning to think about reading', *Educational Research*, 9, 56-92

————— (1983) 'Into print: reading and language growth', in M. Donaldson (ed.), *Early Childhood Development and Education*, Blackwell, Oxford

Robinson, E. J. (1981a) 'The child's understanding of inadequate messages and communication failure: a problem of ignorance or egocentrism?', in W. P. Dickson (ed.), *Children's Oral Communication Skills*, Academic Press, New York

————— (1981b) 'Conversational tactics and the advancement of the child's understanding of referential communication', in W. P. Robinson (ed.), *Communication in Development*, Academic Press, London

————— and Robinson, W. P. (1976a) 'Developmental changes in the child's explanations of communication failure', *Australian Journal of Psychology*, 3, 155-65

————— and ————— (1976b) 'The young child's understanding of communication', *Developmental Psychology*, 12, 328-33

————— and ————— (1977) 'Development in the understanding of causes of success and failure in verbal communication', *Cognition*, 5, 363-78

————— and ————— (1978a) 'Explanations of communication failure and ability to give bad messages', *British Journal of Social and Clinical Psychology*, 17, 219-25

————— and ————— (1978b) 'Development of understanding about communication: message inadequacy and its role in causing communication failure', *Genetic Psychology Monographs*, 98, 233-79

————— and ————— (1980) 'Egocentrism in referential verbal communication', in M. V. Cox (ed.), *Are Young Children Egocentric?*, Batsford, London

———— and ———— (1982) 'The advancement of children's verbal referential communication skills', *International Journal of Behavioural Development*, 5, 329-55

———— and ———— (1983) 'Children's uncertainty about the interpretation of ambiguous messages', *Journal of Experimental Child Psychology*, 35, 81-96

Robinson, W. P. (1978) *Language Management in Education: The Australian Context*, Allen and Unwin, Sydney

Rummelhart, D. E. (1975) 'Notes on a schema for stories', in D. G. Bobrow and A. Collins (eds), *Representation and Understanding*, Academic Press, New York

Ryan, E. B. (1980) 'Metalinguistic development and reading', in F. B. Murray (ed.), *Language Awareness and Reading*, Newark, Delaware

Sachs, J. (1967) 'Recognition memory for syntactic and semantic aspects of connected discourse', *Perception and Psychophysics*, 2, 437-42

Scardamalia, M. and Bereiter, C. (1984) 'Development of strategies in text processing', in H. Mandl (ed.), *Learning and the Comprehension of Text*, Erlbaum, Hillsdale

Schank, R. C. (1975) 'The structure of episodes in memory', in D. G. Bobrow and A. Collins (eds), *Representation and Understanding: Studies in Cognitive Science*, Academic Press, New York

Scholl, D. M. and Ryan, E. B. (1975) 'Child judgements of sentences varying in grammatical complexity', *Journal of Experimental Child Psychology*, 20, 274-85

———— and ———— (1980) 'Development of metalinguistic performance in the early school years', *Language and Speech*, 23, 199-211

Simpson, G. B. *et al.* (1983) 'Encoding and contextual components of word recognition in good and poor readers', *Journal of Experimental Child Psychology*, 35, 161-71

Slackman, E. and Nelson, D. (1984) 'Acquisition of an unfamiliar script in story form by young children', *Child Development*, 55, 329-40

Smith, N. (1973) *The Acquisition of Phonology*, Cambridge University Press, Cambridge

Spielberger, C. D. (1965) 'Theoretical and epistemological issues in verbal conditioning', in S. Rosenberg (ed.), *Directions in Psycholinguistics*, Macmillan, New York

Spiro, R. J. (1980) 'Constructive processes in prose comprehension', in R. J. Spiro *et al.* (eds), *Theoretical Issues in Reading Comprehension*, Erlbaum, Hillsdale

———— and Myers, A. (1979) 'Children's misconceptions about the role of knowledge-based processes in reading comprehension', unpublished paper

————, Tirre, W. C., Freebody, P. and de Loache, J. (1979) 'Reading style etiology and preferences for bottom-up versus top-down processes', unpublished paper

Stauffer, R. G. (1975) *Directing the Reading-Thinking Process*, Harper and Row, New York

Stein, N. L. (1982) 'What's in a story: interpreting the interpretations of story grammars', *Discourse Processes*, 5, 319-35

———— and Glenn, C. G. (1977) 'A developmental study of children's construction of stories', paper presented at the Society for Research in Child Development meeting, New Orleans

———— and ———— (1979) 'An analysis of story comprehension in elementary school children', in R. O. Freedle (ed.), *New Directions in Discourse Processing*, Vol. 2, Ablex, Norwood

———— and ———— (1982) 'Children's concept of time', in W. Friedman (ed.), *The Developmental Psychology of Time*, Academic Press, New York

———— and Trabasso, T. (1984) 'Development of strategies in text processing', in H. Mandl (ed.), *Learning and the Comprehension of Text*, Erlbaum, Hillsdale

Templeton, S. and Spivey, E. M. (1980) 'The concept of word in young children as a function of level of cognitive development', *Research in the Teaching of English*, 14, 265-78

Townsend, M. A. R. (1983) 'Schema-shifting: children's cognitive monitoring of the prose-schema interaction in comprehension', *Journal of Experimental Child Psychology*, 22, 139-49

Trabasso, T. *et al.* (1984) 'Causal cohesion and story coherence', in H. Mandl (ed.), *Learning and the Comprehension of Text*, Erlbaum, Hillsdale

Treiman, R. (1984) 'Individual differences among children in spelling and reading styles', *Journal of Experimental Child Psychology*, 37, 463-77

Tunmer, W. E. and Bowey, J. A. (1983) 'Metalinguistic awareness and reading acquisition', in W. E. Tunmer (ed.), *Metalinguistic Awareness*, Springer, New York

———— and Herriman, M. L. (1983) 'The development of metalinguistic awareness', in W. E. Tunmer (ed.), *Metalinguistic Awareness*, Springer, New York

Van Dijk, J. A. (1973) 'Text grammar and text logic', in J. S. Petofi and H. Rieser (eds), *Studies in Text Grammar*, Dordrecht, Reidel

Van Kleek, A. (1982) 'The emergence of linguistic awareness: a cognitive framework', *Merrill-Palmer Quarterly*, 28, 237-65

Waters, H. S. and Lomenick, T. (1983) 'Levels of organisation in descriptive passages: production, comprehension and recall', *Journal of Experimental Child Psychology*, 35, 391-408

Weaver, P. A. and Dickinson, D. K. (1982) 'Scratching below the surface structure: exploring the usefulness of story grammars', *Discourse Processes*, 5, 225-43

Weir, R. (1962) *Language in the Crib*, Mouton, The Hague

Wells, G. (1978) *Children Learning to Read*, School of Education, University of Bristol, Bristol

————— (1981) *Learning Through Interaction*, Cambridge University Press, Cambridge

Whaley, J. F. (1981) 'Readers' expectations of story structure', *Reading Research Quarterly*, 17, 90-114

Woodford, G. and Fowler, C. A. (1983) 'Perception and use of information in reading', in T. J. Tighe and B. E. Shepp (eds), *Perception Cognition and Development*, Erlbaum, Hillsdale

————— and ————— (1984) 'Differential use of partial information by good and poor readers', *Developmental Review*, 4, 16-35

Zhurova, L. Ye. (1973) 'The development of analysis of words into their sounds by preschool children', in C. A. Ferguson and D. Slobin (eds), *Studies of Child Language Development*, Holt, Rinehart and Winston, New York

Zinck, A. R. (1978) 'Language concepts and language complexity as factors in development of reading readiness', paper presented at the annual meeting of the National Reading Conference, St Petersburg

Chapter 3

Ackerman, B. P. (1978) 'Inferences to speaker belief', *Journal of Experimental Child Psychology*, 26, 92-114

Auzai, Y. and Uchida, N. (1981) 'How do children produce writing?', *Japanese Journal of Educational Psychology*, 27, 323-32

Beard, R. (1984) *Children's Writing in the Primary School*, Hodder and Stoughton, Sevenoaks

Bernstein, B. (1965) 'A socio-linguistic approach to social learning', in J. Gould, *Social Science Survey*, Methuen, London

————— (1971) *Class, Codes and Control*, Vol. 1, Routledge and Kegan Paul, London

————— (1981) 'Codes, modalities and the process of cultural reproduction', *Language and Society*, 8, 327-63

Cambourne, B. L. (1971) 'A Naturalistic Study of Language Performance in Grade 1 Rural and Urban School Children', Monash University, Victoria, Ph.D. thesis

Clough, J. R. (1971) 'An Experimental Investigation of the Effects of a Cognitive Training Programme on Educationally Disadvantaged Children of Pre-school Age', Monash University, Victoria, Ph.D. thesis

Collins, J. I. and Williamson, M. M. (1981) 'Spoken language and semantic abbreviation in writing', *Research in the Teaching of English*, 15, 23-35

Edwards, A. D. (1976) *Language in Culture and Class*, Heinemann, London

Flavell, J. H. *et al.* (1968) *The Development of Role-Taking and Communication Skills in Children*, Wiley, New York

Flower, L. S. and Hayes, J. R. (1981a) 'The pregnant pause: an inquiry into the nature of planning', *Research in the Teaching of English*, 15, 229-43

——— and ——— (1981b) 'A cognitive process theory of writing', *College Composition and Communication*, 32, 365-87

Graves, D. (1975) 'An examination of the writing process of seven year old children', *Research in the Teaching of English*, 9, 227-41

——— (1983) *Writing: Teachers and Children at Work*, Heinemann, Exeter

Inhelder, B. and Piaget, J. (1955) *The Growth of Logical Thinking from Childhood to Adolescence*, Basic Books, New York

——— and ——— (1964) *The Early Growth of Logic in the Child*, Routledge, London

Lawton, D. (1968) *Social Class, Language and Education*, Routledge, London

Lempers, J. D. and Elrod, M. M. (1983) 'Children's appraisal of different sources of referential communication inadequacies', *Child Development*, 54, 509-16

Little, G. (1975) *Form and Function in the Written Language*, University of New South Wales, M.Ed. thesis

——— (1978) 'Content, function, wording and word processing: an approach to language use', unpublished paper, Canberra CAE

Maratsos, M. P. (1973) 'Nonegocentric communication abilities in pre-school children', *Child Development*, 44, 697-700

Menig-Peterson, C. L. (1975) 'The modification of communicative behaviour in pre-school aged children as a function of listener's perspective', *Child Development*, 46, 1015-18

Mosenthal, P. *et al.* (1981) 'How fourth graders develop points of view in classroom writing', *Research in the Teaching of English*, 15, 197-214

——— (1982) 'Towards a paradigm of children's writing competence', *Advances in Reading/Language Research*, 1, 125-54

Nold, E. (1981) 'Revising', in C. Frederiksen *et al.* (eds), *Writing: The Nature, Development and Teaching of Written Communication*, Erlbaum, Hillsdale

Piaget, J. (1926) *The Language and Thought of the Child*, Routledge, London

Robinson, E. J. (1981a) 'The child's understanding of inadequate messages and communication failure: a problem of ignorance or egocentrism?', in W. P. Dickson (ed.), *Children's Oral Communication Skills*, Academic Press, New York

————— (1981b) 'Conversational tactics and the advancement of the child's understanding of referential communication', in W. P. Robinson (ed.), *Communication in Development*, Academic Press, London

Robinson, E. J. and Robinson, W. P. (1976a) 'Developmental changes in the child's explanations of communication failure', *Australian Journal of Psychology*, 3, 155-65

————— and ————— (1976b) 'The young child's understanding of communication', *Developmental Psychology*, 12, 328-33

————— and ————— (1977) 'Development in the understanding of-causes of success and failure in verbal communication', *Cognition*, 5, 363-78

————— and ————— (1978a) 'Explanations of communication failure and ability to give bad messages', *British Journal of Social and Clinical Psychology*, 17, 219-25

————— and ————— (1978b) 'Development of understanding about communication: message inadequacy and its role in causing communication failure', *Genetic Psychology Monographs*, 98, 233-79

————— and ————— (1980) 'Egocentrism in referential verbal communication', in M. V. Cox, *Are Young Children Egocentric?*, Batsford, London

————— and ————— (1982) 'The advancement of children's verbal referential communication skills', *International Journal of Behavioural Development*, 5, 329-55

————— and ————— (1983) 'Children's uncertainty about the interpretation of ambiguous messages', *Journal of Experimental Psychology*, 35, 81-96

Robinson, W. P. (1978) *Language Management in Education: The Australian Context*, Allen and Unwin, Sydney

Shatz, M. and Gelman, R. (1973) 'The development of communication skills: modifications in the speech of young children as a function of listeners', *Monographs of the Society for Research in Child Development*, 38, 1-38

Shaughnessey, M. (1977) *Errors and Expectations*, Oxford University Press, New York

Schumacher, G. M. *et al.* (1984) 'Cognitive activities of beginning and advanced college writers', *Research in the Teaching of English*, 18, 169-78

Toomey, D. (1974) 'Causes of educational disadvantage', *Australian and New Zealand Journal of Sociology*, 10, 31-6

Tough, J. (1977) *Talking and Learning*, Ward Lock, London

Wells, G. (1981) *Learning Through Interaction*, Cambridge University Press, Cambridge

Wilkinson, A. *et al.* (1981) *Assessing Language Development*, Oxford University Press, Oxford

Chapter 4

Alland, A. (1983) *Playing With Form*, Columbia University Press, New York

Booth, D. (1975) *Pattern Painting by the Young Child: A Cognitive-Developmental Approach*, University of Sydney, M.Ed. Thesis

———— (1976) 'Children's non-representational painting', *Australian Journal of Early Childhood*, 1, 26-33

———— (1981) *Aspects of Logico-Mathematical Thinking and Symmetry in the Young Child's Spontaneous Pattern Painting*, La Trobe University, Bundoora, Ph.D. thesis

———— (1982) 'Art education and children's spontaneous pattern painting', *Journal of the Institute of Art Education*, 6, 1-16

———— (1984) 'An experimental study of pattern painting by kindergarten children', *Journal of the Institute of Art Education*, 8, 19-24

Cox, M. V. (1978) 'Spatial depth relationships in young children's drawings', *Journal of Experimental Child Psychology*, 26, 551-4

Davis, A. (1985) 'Conflict between canonicality and array-specificity in young children's drawings', *British Journal of Developmental Psychology*, 3, 363-72

Freeman, N. (1975) 'Do children draw men with arms coming out of the head?', *Nature*, 254, 416-17

———— *et al.* (1977) 'How young children try to plan drawings', in G. E. Butterworth (ed.), *The Child's Representation of the World*, Plenum, New York

———— (1980) *Strategies of Representation in Young Children*, Academic Press, London

Golomb, C. (1983) 'Young children's planning strategies and early principles of spatial organisation in drawing', in D. Rogers and J. A. Sloboda (eds), *The Acquisition of Symbolic Skills*, Plenum, New York

Hess-Behrens, N. (1974) 'The development of the concept of space as observed in children's drawings: a cross-national, cross-cultural study', *Educational Horizons*, 5, 143-52

Ives, S. W. (1984) 'The development of expressivity in children's drawing', *British Journal of Educational Psychology*, 54, 152-9

Kellogg, R. (1970) *Analysing Children's Art*, National Press, Palo Alto

———— and O'Dell, S. (1967) *The Psychology of Children's Art*, Del Mar, San Francisco

Light, P. and Simmons, B. (1983) 'The effects of a communication task upon the representation of depth relationships in young children's drawings', *Journal of Experimental Child Psychology*, 35, 81-92

————— and Foot, T. (1986) 'Partial occlusion in young children's drawings', *British Journal of Developmental Psychology*, 41, 38-48

Luquet, G. H. (1913) *Les Dessins d'un Enfant*, Alcan, Paris

————— (1927) *Le Dessin Enfantin*, Alcan, Paris

Piaget, J. and Inhelder, B. (1948) *The Child's Conception of Space*, Routledge, London

Van Sommers, P. (1983) 'The conservatism of children's drawing strategies', in D. Rogers and J. A. Sloboda (eds), *The Acquisition of Symbolic Skills*, Plenum, New York

————— (1984) *Drawing and Cognition*, Cambridge University Press, Cambridge

Willats, J. (1977) 'How children learn to draw realistic pictures', *Quarterly Journal of Experimental Psychology*, 29, 367-382

Chapter 5

Abdullah, K. B. and Lowell, W. E. (1981) 'The ability of children to generalize selected science concepts', *Journal of Research in Science Teaching*, 18, 547-55

Albert, E. (1978) 'Development of the concept of heat in children', *Science Education*, 62, 389-99

Ammon, S. (1981) 'The understanding of causality in preschool children', *Topics in Language Disorders*, 2, 33-50

Anglin, J. M. (1977) *Word, Object and Conceptual Development*, Norton, New York

Ausubel, D. P. (1963) *The Psychology of Meaningful Learning*, Grune and Stratton, New York

————— (1968) *Educational Psychology: A Cognitive View*, 1st edn, Holt, Rinehart and Winston, New York

Battino, R. (1983) 'Giant atomic and molecular models and other lecture demonstration devices designed for concrete operational students', *Journal of Chemical Education*, 60, 485-90

Bearison, J. D. (1975) 'Induced versus spontaneous attainment of concrete operations and their relation to school achievement', *Journal of Educational Psychology*, 67, 576-80

Bell, B. F. (1981) 'When is an animal not an animal?', *Journal of Biological Education*, 15, 213-18

Berzonsky, M. D. (1971) 'The role of familiarity in children's explanations of physical causality', *Child Development*, 42, 705-15

————— (1974) 'Reflectivity, internality and animistic thinking', *Child Development*, 45, 785-9

Bessemer, D. W. and Smith, E. L. (1972) 'The role of skills analysis in instructional design', in D. W. Bessemer and E. L. Smith (eds), *SWRL Working Papers 1972*, Southwest Regional Lab., Los Alamitos, California

Beveridge, M. (1985) 'The development of young children's understanding of the process of evaporation', *British Journal of Educational Psychology*, 55, 84-90

————— and Davies, M. (1983) 'A picture-sorting approach to the study of childhood animism', *Genetic Psychology Monographs*, 107, 211-31

Billingham, R. E. and Fu, V. R. (1980) 'Animistic thinking between parents and children', *Journal of Psychology*, 105, 35-39

Brainerd, C. J. (1978a) 'Learning research and Piagetian theory', in L. S. Siegel and C. J. Brainerd (eds), *Alternatives to Piaget*, Academic Press, New York

————— (1978b) 'The stage question in cognitive-developmental theory', *Behavioural and Brain Sciences*, 2, 245-57

————— (1978c) *Piaget's Theory of Intelligence*, Prentice-Hall, Englewood Cliffs

————— and Kaszor, P. (1974) 'An analysis of two proposed sources of children's class inclusion errors', *Developmental Psychology*, 10, 633-43

Brown, R. (1958) 'How shall a thing be called?', *Psychological Review*, 65, 14-21

Brumby, M. N. (1982) 'Students' perceptions of the concept of life', *Science Education*, 66, 613-22

Bullock, M. *et al.* (1982) 'The development of causal reasoning', in W. J. Friedman (ed.), *The Developmental Psychology of Time*, Academic Press, New York

————— (1985a) 'Causal reasoning and developmental change over the preschool years', *Human Development*, 28, 169-91

————— (1985b) 'Animism in childhood thinking: a new look at an old question', *Developmental Psychology*, 21, 217-25

————— and Gelman, R. (1979) 'Preschool children's assumptions about cause and effect: temporal ordering', *Child Development*, 50, 89-96

Carbonnel, S. (1982) 'Influence de la signification des objets dans les activités de classification', *Enfance*, 27, 193-210

Clarke, E. (1973) 'What's in a word? On the child's acquisition of semantics in his first language', in T. E. Moore (ed.), *Cognitive Development and the Acquisition of Language*, Academic Press, New York

Comber, M. (1983) 'Concept development in relation to the particulate theory of matter in the middle school', *Research in Science and Technological Education*, 1, 27-39

————— (1985) 'Concept development in relation to the particulate theory of matter in the middle school', *Research in Science and Technological Education*, 1, 27-39

Corrigan, R. (1975) 'A scalogram analysis of the development of the use and comprehension of "because" in children', *Child Development*, 46, 195-201

Deutsche, J. M. (1937) *The Development of Children's Concepts of Causal Relations*, University of Minnesota Press, Minneapolis

Finley, F. N. and Smith, E. L. (1980a) 'Effects of strategy instruction on the learning, use and vertical transfer of strategies', *Science Education*, 64, 367-75

———— and ———— (1980b) 'Student performance resulting from strategy-based instruction in a sequence of conceptually related tasks', *Journal of Research in Science Teaching*, 17, 583-93

Gagné, R. M. (1970) *The Conditions of Learning*, Holt, Rinehart and Winston, New York

———— (1975) *Essentials of Learning for Instruction*, Dryden, Hillsdale

Gelman, R. *et al.* (1983) 'Preschooler's knowledge of animacy', in D. Rogers and J. A. Sloboda (eds), *The Acquisition of Symbolic Skills*, Plenum, New York

Hintzman, D. L. and Ludlum, G. (1980) 'Differential forgetting of prototypes and old instances', *Memory and Cognition*, 8, 378-82

Holland, V. M. and Rohrman, N. L. (1979) 'Distribution of the feature [+ Animate] in the lexicon of the child', *Journal of Psycholinguistic Research*, 8, 367-78

Horton, M. S. and Markman, E. M. (1980) 'Developmental differences in the acquisition of basic and superordinate categories', *Child Development*, 51, 708-19

Huang, I. *et al.* (1945) 'Principles of selection in children's "phenomenistic" explanations', *Journal of Genetic Psychology*, 66, 63-68

Inhelder, B. and Piaget, J. (1955) *The Growth of Logical Thinking from Childhood to Adolescence*, Humanities Press, New York

———— and ———— (1964) *The Early Growth of Logic in the Child*, Routledge, London

Isaacs, S. (1930) *Intellectual Growth in Young Children*, Routledge, London

Kelley, H. H. (1972) 'Causal schemata and the attribution process', in E. E. Jones *et al.* (eds), *Attribution: Perceiving the Causes of Behaviour*, General Learning, Morristown

———— (1973) 'The process of causal attribution', *American Psychologist*, 28, 107-28

Kemler, D. G. (1982) 'Classification in young and retarded children', *Child Development*, 53, 768-79

Kemler, D. G. and Smith, L. B. (1978) 'Is there a development from integrality to separability in perception?', *Journal of Experimental Child Psychology*, 26, 498-507

Kendler, H. H. and Guenther, K. (1980) 'Developmental changes in classificatory behaviour', *Child Development*, 51, 339-48

—— and Kendler, T. S. (1962) 'Vertical and horizontal processes in problem solving', *Psychological Review*, 69, 1-16

—— and —— (1975) 'From discrimination learning to cognitive development', in W. K. Estes (ed.), *Handbook of Learning and Cognitive Processes*, Vol. 1, Erlbaum, Hillsdale

Kendler, T. S. (1983) 'Labelling overtraining and levels of function', in T. J. Tighe and B. E. Shepp (eds), *Perception, Cognition and Development*, Erlbaum, Hillsdale

Klein, C. A. (1982) 'Children's concepts of the Earth and the Sun: a cross cultural study', *Science Education*, 65, 95-107

Kofsky, E. (1966) 'A scalogram study of classificatory development', *Child Development*, 37, 191-204

Koslowski, B. *et al.* (1981) 'Children's beliefs about instances of mechanical and electrical causation', *Journal of Applied Developmental Psychology*, 2, 189-210

Kuhn, D. (1972) 'Mechanisms of change in the development of cognitive structures', *Child Development*, 43, 833-44

—— and Phelps, H. (1976) 'The development of children's comprehension of causal direction', *Child Development*, 47, 248-51

Kun, A. (1977) 'Development of the magnitude-covariation and compensation schemata in ability and effort attributions of performance', *Child Development*, 48, 862-73

—— (1978) 'Evidence for preschoolers' understanding of causal direction in extended causal sequences', *Child Development*, 49, 218-22

—— *et al.* (1974) 'Development of integration processes using ability and effort information to predict outcome', *Developmental Psychology*, 10, 721-32

Langford, P. E. and Berrie, N. (1974) 'Stages in the development of classification concepts', *Archives de Psychologie*, 42, 459-72

Laurendeau, M. and Pinard, A. (1962) *Causal Thinking in the Child*, International Universities Press, New York

Lawrenz, F. (1983) 'Student knowledge of energy issues', *School Science and Mathematics*, 83, 587-93

—— and Dantchek, A. (1986) 'Attitudes towards energy among students in grades 4, 7 and high school', *School Science and Mathematics*, 85, 189-210

Lawton, J. T. and Wanska, S. K. (1979) 'The effects of different types of advance organizers on classification learning', *American Educational Research Journal*, 16, 223-39

Lewis, M. M. (1963) *Language, Thought and Personality in Infancy and Childhood*, Basic Books, New York

Looft, W. R. (1973) 'Animistic thought in children: understanding of "living" across its associated attributes', *Journal of Genetic Psychology*, 124, 235-40
——— (1974) 'Animistic thought in children', *Journal of Genetic Psychology*, 124, 235-40
——— and Bartz, W. H. (1969) 'Animism revived', *Psychological Bulletin*, 71, 1-19
——— and Charles, D. C. (1969) 'Modification of the life concept in children', *Developmental Psychology*, 1, 445
Lowell, W. E. (1977) 'An empirical study of a model of abstract learning', *Science Education*, 61, 229-42
——— (1979) 'A study of hierarchical classification in concrete and abstract thought', *Journal of Research in Science Teaching*, 16, 255-62
——— (1980) 'The development of hierarchical classification skills in science', *Journal of Research in Science Teaching*, 17, 425-33
Lucas, A. M. *et al.* (1979) 'Schoolchildren's criteria for "alive": a content analysis approach', *Journal of Psychology*, 103, 103-12
Mali, G. B. and Howe, A. (1979) 'Development of Earth and gravity concepts among Nepali children', *Science Education*, 63, 685-91
Markman, E. M. (1978) 'Empirical versus logical solutions to part-whole comparison problems', *Child Development*, 49, 168-77
——— (1979) 'Classes and collections', *Cognition*, 8, 227-41
——— (1983) 'Two different kinds of hierarchical organisation', in E. K. Scholnick (ed.), *New Trends in Conceptual Representation: Challenges to Piaget's Theory?*, Erlbaum, Hillsdale
——— and Siebert, J. (1976) 'Classes and collections', *Cognitive Psychology*, 8, 561-77
——— *et al.* (1980) 'Classes and collections: principles of organisation in the learning of hierarchical relations', *Cognition*, 8, 227-41
——— *et al.* (1981) 'The standard object-sorting task as a measure of conceptual organization', *Developmental Psychology*, 17, 115-17
Medin, D. L. (1983) 'Structural principles in categorization', in T. J. Tighe and B. E. Shepp (eds), *Perception, Cognition and Development*, Erlbaum, Hillsdale
——— and Schaffer, M. M. (1978) 'Context theory of classification learning', *Psychological Review*, 85, 207-38
——— and Smith, E. E. (1981) 'Strategies and classification learning', *Journal of Experimental Psychology: Human Learning and Memory*, 7, 241-53
Mervis, C. B. and Crisafi, M. A. (1982) 'Order of acquisition of subordinate , basic- and superordinate-level categories', *Child Development*, 53, 258-66
Modgil, S. and Modgil, C. (1976a) *Piagetian Research: Compilation and Commentary*, Vol. 2, NFER, Slough

———— and ———— (1976b) *Piagetian Research: Compilation and Commentary*, Vol. 3, NFER, Slough

Nass, M. L. (1956) 'The effects of three variables on children's concepts of physical causality', *Journal of Abnormal and Social Psychology*, 53, 191-6

Neimark, E. E. (1974) 'Natural language concepts: additional evidence', *Child Development*, 45, 508-11

Nelson, K. J. (1974) 'Variations in children's concepts by age and category', *Child Development*, 45, 577-84

———— et al. (1978) 'Early lexicons: what do they mean?', *Child Development*, 49, 960-8

Novak, J. D. (1977) 'An alternative to Piagetian psychology for science and mathematics education', *Science Education*, 61, 324-51

Nussbaum, J. (1979) 'Children's conceptions of the Earth as a cosmic body: a cross-age study', *Science Education*, 63, 83-93

———— and Novak, J. D. (1976) 'An assessment of children's concepts of the Earth using structured interviews', *Science Education*, 60, 535-50

———— and Sharoni-Dagan, N. (1983) 'Changes in second grade children's preconceptions about the Earth as a cosmic body resulting from a short series of audio-tutorial lessons', *Science Education*, 67, 99-114

Osborne, R. J. (1982) *Investigating Children's Ideas About Electric Current Using An Interview-About-Instances Procedure*, University of Waikato, New Zealand

———— (1983) 'Towards modifying children's ideas about electric current', *Research in Science and Technological Education*, 1, 73-81

———— and Gilbert, J. K. (1980) 'A method for investigating concept understanding in science', *European Journal of Science Education*, 2, 311-21

———— and Freyberg, P. (1985) *Learning in Science: the Implications of Children's Science*, Heinemann, Auckland

———— et al. (1981) *Video: Electric Current*, Paper No. 51, Learning in Science Project, University of Waikato, New Zealand

Piaget, J. (1929) *The Child's Conception of the Word*, Routledge, London

———— (1930) *The Child's Conception of Physical Causality*, Routledge, London

———— (1967) *Six Psychological Studies*, Random House, New York

———— et al. (1968) *Epistémologie et Psychologie de la Fonction*, Presses Universitaires de France, Paris

———— (1971) *Les Explications Causales*, Presses Universitaires de France, Paris

———— and Inhelder, B. (1941) *Le Developpement des Quantités Chez l'Enfant*, Delachaux et Nieslé, Neûchatel and Paris

Posner, M. I. and Keele, S. W. (1968) 'On the genesis of abstract ideas' *Journal of Experimental Psychology*, 77, 353-63

Rodrigues, D. M. A. P. (1980) 'Notions of physical laws in childhood', *Science Education*, 64, 59-84

Rosch, E. H. (1973) 'On the internal structure of perception and semantic categories', in T. E. Moore(ed.), *Cognitive Development and the Acquisition of Language*, Academic Press, New York

————— (1978) 'Principles of categorization', in E. Rosch and B. B. Lloyd (eds), *Cognition and Categorization*, Erlbaum, Hillsdale

————— *et al.* (1976) 'Basic objects in natural categories', *Cognitive Psychology*, 8, 382-439

Rosenthal, T. L. and Zimmerman, B. J. (1978) *Social Learning and Cognition*, Academic Press, New York

Rosser, R. A. and Horan, P. F. (1982) 'Acquisition of multiple classification and seriation from the observation of models', *Child Development*, 53, 1229-32

Rowell, J. A. and Dawson, C. J. (1977a) 'Teaching about floating and sinking: an attempt to link cognitive psychology with classroom practice', *Science Education*, 61, 243-51

————— and ————— (1977b) 'Teaching about floating and sinking: further studies toward closing the gap between cognitive psychology and classroom practice', *Science Education*, 61, 527-40

Ryman, D. (1977) 'Teaching methods, intelligence and gender factors in pupil achievement on a classification task', *Journal of Research in Science Teaching*, 14, 401-9

Saltz, E. *et al.* (1972) 'The development of natural language concepts', *Child Development*, 43, 1191-1202

Sato, Y. (1978) 'Transfer of concepts and grouping strategy in children', *Japanese Psychological Research*, 20, 84-92

Saxby, L. and Anglin, J. M. (1983) 'Children's sorting of objects from categories of differing levels of generality', *Journal of Genetic Psychology*, 143, 123-37

Sedgwick, P. P. *et al.* (1978) 'A comparison of changes in children's concepts of life with the development of relevant criteria in Australian science curriculum materials', *Research in Science Education*, 8, 195-203

Sedlak, A. J. and Kurtz, S. T. (1981) 'A review of children's use of causal inference principles', *Child Development*, 52, 759-84

Selman, R. L. *et al.* (1982) 'Concrete operational thought and the emergence of the concept of unseen force in children's theories of electromagnetism and gravity', *Science Education*, 66, 181-94

Shaklee, S. and Paszek, D. (1985) 'Covariation judgement', *Child Development*, 56, 1229-40

Sharp, K. C. *et al.* (1985) 'Children's judgment and reasoning about aliveness: effects of object, age and cultural-social background', *Merrill-Palmer Quarterly*, 31, 47-65

Shultz, T. R. and Mendelson, R. (1975) 'The use of covariation as a principle of causal analysis', *Child Development*, 46, 394-9

—————— and Ravinsky, F. B. (1977) 'Similarity as a principle of causal inference', *Child Development*, 48, 1552-8

—————— *et al.* (1986) 'Selection of causal rules', *Child Development*, 57, 143-52

Siegler, R. S. (1975) 'Defining the locus of developmental differences in children's causal reasoning', *Journal of Experimental Child Psychology*, 20, 512-25

—————— (1976) 'The effects of simple necessity and sufficiency relationships on children's causal inferences', *Child Development*, 47, 1058-63

—————— and Liebert, R. M. (1974) 'Effects of contiguity, regularity and age on children's causal inferences', *Developmental Psychology*, 10, 574-9

Smith, E. E. *et al.* (1974) 'Structure and process in semantic memory: a featural model for semantic decisions', *Psychological Review*, 81, 214-41

Smith, L. B. (1979) 'Perceptual development and category generalisation', *Child Development*, 50, 705-15

—————— (1983) 'Development of classification: the use of similarity and dimensional relations', *Journal of Experimental Child Psychology*, 36, 150-78

—————— and Kemler, D. G. (1977) 'Developmental trends in free classification', *Journal of Experimental Psychology*, 24, 279-98

—————— and —————— (1978) 'Levels of experienced dimensionality in children and adults', *Cognitive Psychology*, 10, 502-32

Sneider, C. and Pulos, S. (1983) 'Children's cosmographies: understanding the Earth's shape and gravity', *Science Education*, 67, 205-21

Sophian, C. and Huber, A. (1984) 'Early developments in children's causal judgments', *Child Development*, 55, 512-26

Stavy, R. *et al.* (1974) *Heat: Teacher's Guide and Student Manual Edition* (in Hebrew), Tel Aviv University Press, Tel Aviv

—————— and Berkowitz, B. (1980) 'Cognitive conflict as a basis for teaching quantitative aspects of the concept of temperature', *Science Education*, 64, 679-92

—————— and Stachel, D. (1985) 'Children's conceptions of changes in the states of matter', *Archives de Psychologie*, 53, 331-44

Strauss, S. *et al.* (1977) 'The child's development of the concept of temperature', unpublished paper, Tel Aviv University

Sugarman, S. (1983) *Children's Early Thought*, Cambridge University Press, Cambridge

Sugimura, T. (1978) 'Effects of pretraining concept names on a conceptual sorting task in children', *Japanese Psychological Research*, 20, 29-38

Trowbridge, J. E. and Mintzes, J. J. (1985) 'Students' alternative conceptions of animals and animal classification', *School Science and Mathematics*, 85, 304-13

Tunmer, W. E. (1985) 'The acquisition of the sentient-nonsentient distinction', *Child Development*, 56, 989-99

Tversky, A. (1977) 'Features of similarity', *Psychological Review*, 84, 327-52

Urevbu, A. O. (1984) 'Teaching concepts of energy to Nigerian children in the 7-11 year old age range', *Journal of Research in Science Teaching*, 21, 255-67

Vincenzo, J. P. de and Kelly, F. J. (1984) 'Does Piaget's graphic collections (stage 1 classification) exist?', *Journal of Genetic Psychology*, 144, 265-77

Whitehead, A. N. (1938) *Modes of Thought*, Cambridge University Press, Cambridge

Williamson, P. A. (1981) 'The effects of methodology and level of development on children's animistic thought', *Journal of Genetic Psychology*, 138, 159-74

Winer, G. A. (1980) 'Class-inclusion reasoning in children: a review of the empirical literature', *Child Development*, 51, 309-28

Wolfinger, D. M. (1982) 'Effect of science teaching on the young child's concept of Piagetian physical causality: animism and dynamism', *Journal of Research in Science Teaching*, 19, 595-602

Za'rour, G. I. (1976) 'Interpretation of natural phenomena by Lebanese school children', *Science Education*, 60, 277-87

Chapter 6

Acredolo, C. (1981) 'The acquisition of conservation', *Human Development*, 24, 120-37

————— (1982) 'Conservation and non-conservation: alternative explanations', in C. J. Brainerd (ed.), *Children's Logical and Mathematical Cognition*, Springer-Verlag, New York

Anderson, G. L. (1949) 'A comparison of the outcomes of instruction under two theories of learning', in E. J. Swenson *et al.* (eds), *Learning Theory in School Situations*, University of Minneapolis Press, Minneapolis

Ashcraft, M. H. (1982) 'The development of mental arithmetic: the chronometric approach', *Developmental Review*, 2, 213-36

————— and Battaglia, J. (1978) 'Cognitive arithmetic: evidence for retrieval and decision processes in mental addition', *Journal of Experimental Psychology: Human Learning and Memory*, 4, 527-38

Ashlock R. B. (1982) *Error Patterns in Computation*, Charles E. Merrill, Columbus

Brainerd, C. J. (1973a) 'Mathematical and behavioural foundations of number', *Journal of General Psychology*, 88, 221-81

———— (1973b) 'The origins of number concepts', *Scientific American*, 228, 101-9

———— (1975) 'Structures-of-the-whole and elementary education', *American Educational Research Journal*, 12, 369-78

———— (1979) *The Origins of Number Concepts*, Praeger, New York

———— (1983) 'Young children's mental arithmetic errors', *Child Development*, 54, 812-830

Brannin, J. R. (1983) 'Cognitive factors in children's arithmetic errors', in D. Rogers and J. A. Sloboda (eds), *The Acquisition of Symbolic Skills*, Plenum, New York

Briars, D. J. and Larkin, J. H. (1984) 'An integrated model of skill in solving elementary word problems', *Cognition and Instruction*, 1, 245-96

Brown, J. S. and Burton, R. R. (1978) 'Diagnostic models for procedural bugs in basic mathematical skills', *Cognitive Science*, 2, 155-92

Brownell, W. A. and Chazal, C. B. (1935) 'The effects of premature drill in third grade arithmetic', *Journal of Educational Research*, 29, 27-28

———— and Moser, H. E. (1949) *Meaningful versus Mechanical Learning*, Duke University Press, Durham

Bruner, J. S. (1966) 'On the conservation of liquids', in J. S. Bruner *et al.* (eds), *Studies in Cognitive Growth*, Wiley, New York

Bryant, P. E. (1974) *Perception and Understanding in Young Children*, Methuen, London

Carpenter, T. P., Hiebert, J. and Moser, J. M. (1983) 'The effect of instruction on children's solution of addition and subtraction word problems', *Educational Studies in Mathematics*, 14, 55-72

———— and Moser, J. M. (1982) 'The development of addition and subtraction problem-solving skills', in T. P. Carpenter *et al.* (eds), *Addition and Subtraction: A Cognitive Perspective*, Erlbaum, Hillsdale

Copeland, R. W. (1974) *How Children Learn Mathematics*, Macmillan, New York

Cox, L. S. (1975) 'Systematic errors in the four vertical algorithms in normal and handicapped populations', *Journal for Research in Mathematics Education*, 6, 202-20

Cronbach, L. J. and Snow, R. E. (1977) *Aptitudes and Instructional Methods*, Irvington, New York

———— and Webb, N. (1975) 'Between-class and within-class effects in a reported aptitude X treatment interaction: reanalysis of a study by G. L. Anderson', *Journal of Educational Psychology*, 67, 717-24

Davis, R. B. and McKnight, C. (1980) 'The influence of semantic content on algorithmic behaviour', *Journal of Mathematical Behaviour*, 3, 39-79

Davydov, V. V. and Andronov, V. P. (1981) *Psychological Conditions for the Origination of Ideal Actions*, Research and Development Center for Individualized Schooling, University of Wisconsin, Wisconsin

Dienes, Z. P. (1960) *Building Up Mathematics*, Hutchinson, New York

———— (1966) *Mathematics in the Primary School*, Macmillan, London

Fehr, H. F. (1966) 'The teaching of mathematics in the elementary school', in H. J. Klausmeier and C. W. Harris (eds), *Analysis of Concept Learning*, Academic Press, New York

Fischbein, E., Tirosh, D. and Hess, P. (1979) 'The intuition of infinity', *Educational Studies in Mathematics*, 10, 1-63

Fuson, K. C. (1981) 'An analysis of the counting-on solution procedure in addition', in T. P. Carpenter *et al.* (eds), *Addition and Subtraction, A Cognitive Perspective*, Erlbaum, Hillsdale

————, Richards, J. and Briars, D. J. (1982) 'The acquisition and elaboration of the number word sequence', in C. J. Brainerd (ed.), *Children's Logical and Mathematical Cognition*, Springer-Verlag, New York

Gagné, R. M. (1983) 'Some issues in the psychology of mathematics instruction', *Journal for Research in Mathematics Education*, 14, 7-18

Gelman, R. (1972) 'Logical capacity of very young children: number invariance rules', *Child Development*, 43, 75-90

———— and Gallistel, C. R. (1978) *The Child's Understanding of Number*, Harvard University Press, Cambridge, Massachusetts

Gibson, E. J. (1969) *Principles of Perceptual Learning and Development*, Van Nostrand, New York

Ginsburg, H. P. (1977) *Children's Arithmetic: the Learning Process*, Van Norstrand, New York

Greaves, B. (1983) 'The numeral system practice effect on arithmetical computation at the basic level of arithmetical competence', *Research in Mathematics Education in Australia*, 1, 7-13

Groen, G. J. and Poll, M. (1973) 'Subtraction and the solution of open sentence problems', *Journal of Experimental Child Psychology*, 16, 292-302

Halford, G. S. and Boyle, F. M. (1984) 'Do young children understand conservation of number?', *Child Development*, 56, 165-76

Hall, D. E. (1966) *The Ability of Intermediate Grade Children to Deal with Aspects of Quantitative Judgement*, Boston University, Massachusetts, Ph.D. thesis

Hollander, S. K. (1978) 'A literature review: thought processes employed in the solution of verbal arithmetic problems', *School Science and Mathematics*, 78, 327-34

Houlihan, D. M. and Ginsburg, H. P. (1981) 'The addition methods of first and second grade children', *Journal for Research in Mathematics Education*, 12, 95-106

Jerman, M. (1973-74) 'Problem length as a structural variable in verbal arithmetic problems', *Educational Studies in Mathematics*, 5, 109-23

———— and Rees, R. (1972) 'Predicting the relative difficulty of verbal arithmetic problems', *Educational Studies in Mathematics*, 4, 306-23

Kingma, J. and Koops, W. (1981) 'On the sequentiality of ordinality and cardinality', *International Journal of Behavioural Development*, 4, 391-402

Kintsch, W. and Greeno, J. G. (1985) 'Understanding and solving word arithmetic problems', *Psychological Review*, 92, 109-29

Klahr, D. and Wallace, J. G. (1976) *Cognitive Development: An Information-Processing View*, Erlbaum, Hillsdale

Langford, P. E. (1974) 'Development of concepts of infinity and limit in mathematics', *Archives de Psychologie*, 42, 311-22

———— (1979) *Beyond Piaget: Recent Theories of Concept Development and Their Significance for Teaching*, School of Education, La Trobe University, Bundoora

———— (1981) 'A longitudinal study of the development of logical laws in arithmetic and Boolean algebra', *Educational Psychology*, 1, 119-39

———— (1986a) 'Solving arithmetical word problems: thinking in the head versus thinking on the table', *Educational Studies in Mathematics*, 17, 193-99

———— (1986b) 'A comparison of individualised with traditional arithmetic instruction', *Research in Mathematics Education in Australia*, 3(2), 1-8

Lifschitz, M. and Langford, P. E. (1977) 'The role of counting and measurement in conservation learning', *Archives de Psychologie*, 45, 1-14

Lovell, K. (1971) *The Growth of Understanding in Mathematics*, Holt, Rinehart and Winston, New York

McConnell, T. M. (1934) 'Discovery vs authoritative identification in the learning of children', *University of Iowa Studies in Education*, 9, 11-62

Michie, S. (1985) 'Development of absolute and relative concepts of number in preschool children', *Developmental Psychology*, 21, 247-52

Modgil, S. and Modgil, C. (1976) *Piagetian Research: Compilation and Commentary*, Vol 2, NFER, Slough

Moore, C. *et al.* (1984) 'Precocious conservation in context: the solution of quantity tasks by nonquantitative strategies', *Journal of Experimental Child Psychology*, 38, 1-6

Nelson, N. Z. (1967) *The Effect of Teaching Estimation on Arithmetic Achievement in the 4th and 6th Grade*, University Pittsburg, Pennsylvania, Ph.D. thesis

Nelson, T. M. and Bartley, S. M. (1961) 'Numerosity, number, arithmetization and psychology', *Philosophy of Science*, 28, 178-203

Parkman, J. M. (1972) 'Temporal aspects of simple multiplication and comparison', *Journal of Experimental Psychology*, 95, 437-44

Paul, D. R. (1971) *The Ability to Estimate in Mathematics*, Columbia University, New York, Ph.D. thesis

Piaget, J. (1941) *The Child's Conception of Number*, Humanities Press, New York

———— (1963) 'Defense de l'épistemologie génétique', in E. Beth *et al.* (eds), *Études d'Épistémologie Génétique*, Vol. 15, *La Filiation des Structures*, Presses Universitaires de France

———— (1967) 'Mathématiques: Les donnés génétiques', in *Encyclopédia de la Pleiade*, Gallimard, Paris

————, Inhelder, B. and Szeminska, A. (1960) *The Child's Conception of Geometry*, trans. E. A. Lunzer, Routledge, London

Potter, M. C. and Levy, E. I. (1968) 'Spatial enumeration without counting', *Child Development*, 39, 265-73

Resnick L. B. and Ford, W. W. (1981) *The Psychology of Mathematics for Instruction*, Erlbaum, Hillsdale

Reys, R. E., Rybolt, J. F., Bestgen, B. J. and Wyatt, J. W. (1982) 'Processes used by good computational estimators', *Journal for Research in Mathematics Education*, 13, 183-201

Riley, M. S. (1981) *Conceptual and Procedural Knowledge in Development*, University of Pittsburgh, Pennsylvania, M.A. thesis

————, Greeno, J. G. and Heller, J. I. (1983) 'Development of children's problem-solving ability in arithmetic', in H. P. Ginsburg (ed.), *The Development of Mathematical Thinking*, Academic Press, New York

Rubenstein, R. N. (1985) 'Computational estimation and related mathematical skills', *Journal for Research in Mathematics Education*, 16, 106-19

Schoen, H. L., Friesen, C. D., Jarrett, J. A. and Urbatsch, T. D. (1981) 'Instruction in estimating solutions of whole number computations', *Journal for Research in Mathematics Education*, 12, 165-78

Secanda, W. G., Fuson, K. C. and Hall, J. W. (1983) 'The transition from counting-all to counting-on in addition', *Journal for Research in Mathematics Education*, 14, 47-57

Sommerville, S. C. and Bryant, P. E. (1985) 'Young children's use of spatial co-ordinates', *Child Development*, 56, 604-13

Sutherlin, W. N. (1977) *The Pocket Calculator: Its Effect on the Acquisition of Decimal Estimation Skills of Intermediate Grade Levels*, University of Oregon, Ph.D. thesis

Thiele, C. L. (1938) *The Contribution of Generalisation to the Learning of Addition Facts*, Teachers College, Columbia University, New York

Wallach, L. (1969) 'On the bases of conservation', in D. Elkind and J. H. Flavell (eds), *Studies in Cognitive Development*, Oxford University Press, New York

Wolters, M. A. D. (1983) 'The part-whole schema and arithmetical problems', *Educational Studies in Mathematics*, 14, 127-38

INDEX

To locate references to an author not in the main text, consult the bibliographies at the end of the book. Then consult this index and the Further Reading and Notes sections to that chapter to find the exact location.

Abdullah, K. B. 1981
abstract rationale 93-5
Ackerman, B. P. 32
Acredolo, C. 78-9
Adams, M. J. 17
Agnew, A. T. 23
Albert, E. 68
algorithms 91-6
alive, concept of 63-4
Alland, A. 47
Andronov, V. P. 87
angles 76
animal, concept of 63-4
animism 59, 63-4
approximation, in arithmetic 96-8
Aristotle 59, 65
arithmetic 86-98
arithmetical word problems 88-91
artificialism 59, 67
Ashlock, R. B. 96
associations 7-9, 56-8, 61
atoms 72-3
audiences, for communication 31-4
Ausubel, D. 2, 12, 67

Bartlett, F. C. 18
Battino, R. 72
Bearison, J. D. 67
Bell, B. F. 64
Bereiter, C. 24
Berkowitz, B. 69
Bernstein, B. 32
Billingham, R. E. 64
Black, J. B. 19
Boolean logic 76
Booth, D. 40, 42, 47-50

Brainerd, C. J. 7, 81-4
Bransford, J. D. 18
Brown, A. L. 20, 21
Brown, J. S. 96
Brownell, W. A. 94-5
Bruner, J. 2, 79
Bryant, P. E. 79
Burton, R. R. 96

Cancelli, A. 20
cardinal numbers 80-4
Carpenter, T. P. 89, 90
Case, R. 6
causality 58-64
Chall, J. S. 23
Chomsky, N. 18
circuits, electrical 70-2
classification 54-8
Clay, M. 22
coding, for audiences 31-4
Collins, J. I. 33
Comber, M. 73
communication 8-10
compensation, and conservation 78
complexity 5
comprehension, of stories 19-21
computational procedures 91-8
concrete operations 4-6
conservation 77-80
constituent concepts 5
construction of schema 18
Cook, B. 20
Cook, L. K. 23, 24
cosmography 64-6
counting 79-88, 93-5
covariance, and causality 60-2
Cox, M. V. 46

cross-classification 55-7
cross-cultural studies 39-40, 47
Cruse, D. F. 20
currents, electric 70-2

Davydov, V. V. 87
Day, H. D. 22
Day, K. C. 22
debugging, of computational procedures 96
density 67
depth, in drawings 44-6
Deutsche, J. M. 63
Dickinson, D. K. 21
Dienes, Z. P. 12, 85
directed reading and thinking activity 23
Dooling, D. J. 18
Downing, J. 22, 23
drawing, 36-53
dynamism 59

earth, concept of 65-6
egocentrism 9, 31-4
Ehri, L. C. 22
Elbow, P. 29
electricity 70-2
electrons 71
Elrod, M. M. 33
energy, 67-70

Fehr, H. F. 86, 94
finalism 59
Fischbein, E. 76
Flavell, J. 32
floating 66-7
Ford, W. W. 86, 94
Fowler, C. A. 17
Fraisse, P. 20, 21
Freebody, P. 17
Freeman, N. 40, 42, 48
Fu, V. R. 64
Fuson, K. C. 86-8

Gagné, R. M. 2-3, 13, 93
Gallistel, C. R. 82

Gelman, R. 79, 82
geometry 76
Gibson, E. J. 78-9, 80
Gilbert, J. K. 69, 71
Ginsburg, H. P. 91
Goodman, K. 9, 15-16
Gowin, D. B. 14
graphic collections 55
graphophonic cues 16
Graves, D. 28, 29, 35
gravity 64-6
Greaves, B. 94
Greeno, J. G. 89

Halford, G. S. 6
Hall, J. W. 87
Harding, L. M. 17
heat 66-70
Heller, J. I. 89
Hess-Behrens, N. 34, 40
Hiebert, E. H. 22
hierarchical classification 55, 57-8
hierarchies, and story structure 18-20
hierarchy of skills 2-4, 13
Hintzman, D. L. 74
Houlihan, D. M. 92
Huang, I. 59
Huggins, A. W. F. 17

identity, and conservation 78
Inhelder, B. 36-47, 55, 57, 66-7, 72
intellectual realism, in drawing 38-9, 43, 49
interactionist, view of reading 25
Isaacs, S. 59

Johns, J. L. 22
Johnson, M. K. 18
Johnson, N. S. 18, 19, 20

Karplus, R. 10-11, 54, 73
Kelley, H. H. 61
Kellogg, R. 47-8
Kingma, J. 782
Kintsch, W. 19
Klahr, D. 79

Koblinski, S. A. 20
Koops, W. 82
Koslowski, B. 71
Kun, A. 62

Lachman, R. 18
Langford, P. E. 5, 76, 77, 79, 80, 95
language experience approach 16
Laurendeau, M. 59
Lawrenz, F. 70
Lawton, J. T. 58
learning, mechanisms of 7-12, 56-8, 61, 68-9
Lempers, J. D. 33
Lesgold, A. M. 17
Lifschitz, M. 79, 80
Light, P. 47
Little, G. 30
Lomenick, T. 19
Lovell, K. 86
Lowell, W. E. 57, 81
Ludlum, G. 74
Luquet, G. H. 39

McConaughy, M. 21
magical thinking 59-64
Mandler, J. M. 18, 19, 20
Mayer, R. E. 23, 24
Mayfield, M. I. 23
Mendelson, R. 61
Menig-Peterson, C. L. 32
mental models 11-12, 73
Michie, S. 82
Modgil, C. 67, 77
Modgil, S. 67, 77
molecules 72-5
moon, concept of 64-6
Mosenthal, P. 34
Moser, H. E. 94-5
multibase 85-6

natural categories 56
natural law 58-60
Nelson, N. Z. 98
non-representational art 47-53

Novak, J. D. 14, 65, 67
number concepts 80
number systems 85-6

oblique projection 44, 46
occlusion, and drawing 45-7
oracy 25
ordinal number 80-4
organisation, in writing 30-1
orthogonal projection 45
Osborne, R. J. 69, 71

painting 36-53
parental influence 64
Pascual-Leone, J. 6
pattern making 48-51
Perfetti, S. A. 17
perspective, and drawing 44-6
phenomenism 59
Piaget, J. 1-3, 12-13, 20, 21, 32, 36-47, 51, 54-73, 76-84, 99
Pinard, A. 59
Prawat, R. S. 20
print, concepts of 21-3
process writing 28-35
prototypes 56

rationale, for computations 93-6
reading 15-27
reading process 15-17, 24-5
recall, of stories 19-21
recognition, of stories 19-21
Reid, J. F. 22
Riley, M. S. 89
representational art 36-47
Resnick, L. B. 86, 94
reversibility, and conservation 78
Reys, R. E. 97-8
Robinson, E. J. 32, 33
Robinson, W. 32

Scardamalia, M. 24
schemas 11-12, 18-20, 41, 61-4
Schoen, H. L. 98
Schultz, T. R. 61
scribble 47-9

Secanda, W. G. 87
semantic cues 16
sequence, in drawing 41-2
set theory 76
sight vocabulary 16-17, 25
Simmons, B. 47
sinking 66-7
Smith, E. E. 56
space, and drawing 36-47
states of matter 72
Stauffer, R. G. 23
Stavy, R. 68-9
strategies 11
strategies, of reading 23-4
Strauss, S. 68
story, concepts of 17-21, 25
subitising 77-85
sun, concept of 64-6
syntactic cues 16
synthetic incapacity 37-8

temperature 68-9
temporal precedence principle 60-2
Tirre, W. C. 17
topology 49
Tough, J. 33
transductive thinking 59

Urevbu, A. O. 69, 70

Van Dijk, T. A. 19
Van Sommers, P. 41
vertical oblique projection 44
visual realism, in drawing 39
volume 67

Wallace, J. G. 79
Wanska, S. K. 58
Waters, H. S. 19
Weaver, P. A. 21
weight 67
Wells, G. 25
Whaley, J. F. 20
Whitehead, A. N. 59
Wilenski, R. 19

Wilkinson, A. 30, 31
Willats, J. 44-6
Williamson, M. M. 33
Wolfinger, D. M. 64
Woodford, G. 17
work 67-70
working memory 6-7
writing 28-35